COLLECTOR'S GUIDE TO

Glass Banks

IDENTIFICATION AND VALUES

Charles V. Reynolds

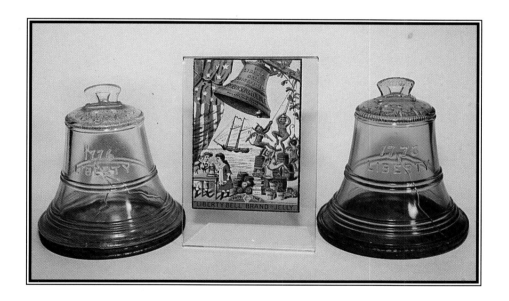

COLLECTOR BOOKS

A Division of Schroeder Publishing Co., Inc.

The current values in this book should be used only as a guide. They are not intended to set prices, which vary from one section of the country to another. Auction prices as well as dealer prices vary greatly and are affected by condition and demand. Neither the author nor the publisher assumes responsibility for any losses which might be incurred as a result of consulting this guide.

On the Cover
Gattuso Rabbit, $300.00 – 600.00.
Jumbo Elephant, $1,000.00+.
Change for the Baby, $75.00 – 150.00.
Cobalt Piggy Bank, $35.00 – 75.00.
Social Security Milk, $35.00 – 75.00.
Pink Shmoo, $300.00 – 600.00.
Snow Bubble Bank, $1,000.00+.

Cover design: Beth Summers
Book design: Holly C. Long

Searching For A Publisher?

We are always looking for knowledgeable people considered experts within their fields. If you feel that there is a real need for a book on your collectible subject and have a large comprehensive collection, contact Collector Books.

Collector Books
P.O. Box 3009
Paducah, KY 42002-3009
www.collectorbooks.com

Contents

Dedication

This book is dedicated to the memories of Marvin Johnson and Harold Shade, two pioneer glass bank collectors who began collecting glass banks over 30 years ago. I traded glass banks and glass bank information with these two gentlemen in the late 1960s and early 1970s. Both of these men had a keen interest in glass banks of all types. Both have passed away.

"Glass banks are beautiful!"
Harold Shade

Acknowledgments

The following collectors, dealers, and club members from the SBCCA and the CCC of America contributed information, banks, or photographs for this project.

David Abbey
Mike Baldwin
Jeff Bradford
Carl Camillo, Jr.
Charles and Dottie Carpenter
Brian Cleary
Bruce Cline
Doug Deszo
Larry Egelhoff
Mark Ehlers
Ken Etheridge
Don & Joann Gifford
Larry Goldman

Tom Hagan
John Haley
Gail Hammer
Bonnie and Jim Hare
Jim Kirk
Peter Maine
Jean Morris
Joyce and Walter O'Neal
Bob and Shirley Peirce
Lee and Rose Poirier
Jason and Jami Reynolds
  (computer setup)

Judy Reynolds
  (for not filing for divorce)
Connie and Joyce Riegner
Ralph Riovo
Dick Soukup
Ginny and Bob Stigers
Lillian Stone
Carl White
Terry Whitmeyer
Guy Williams
Hampton Williams

Preface

My wife Judy and I have collected glass banks since the early 1960s. When we gathered a collection of over 200, we thought we had almost all of them. I contacted and dealt with the few known glass bank collectors and became more interested in trading information and banks. Knowledge about what existed at that time was very limited. Then for about 10 years there seemed like there was nothing new to add to the collection. Next came the *Glass Bank Newsletter*, which represents a group of collectors within the Still Bank Collectors Club of America. More information became available, new finds were made, and glass bank collecting resumed. Then came the explosion with the Internet. Our collection has reached almost 1,000 glass banks and is still growing.

This book started out as a small project for the SBCCA to publish but soon grew into a major project that needed a publishing company.

Hopefully you will find this book educational and informative. I consider this to be a work in progress and hope to update it with new finds and information in the years to come. If at any time you can add information to this work, please contact the author.

Introduction

The purpose of this book is to identify as many different glass banks as possible, to photograph and place them in the categories that suit each type of glass bank collecting interest. The banks will have a sequential number in each category so that new finds may be added easily to future updates of the book.

There are fourteen categories to identify every type of glass and part glass bank produced.

Over the past 30 years some figural glass bottles without slots have been accepted into glass bank collections. Even though any glass bottle could be used as a bank with the unique features of a removable trap (lid) and transparent walls to view the coins, the figural glass bottles without slots shown in this work are accepted by age and provenance. Also included are some glass candy containers found with slots, that are not usually known to have slots. You, as a collector of glass banks, may choose to collect those that appeal to you.

Glass Bank History

The earliest glass banks were produced by the Boston and Sandwich Glass Works between 1825 and 1840. These banks range from simple glass balls with a pulled slot to very ornate, as tall as 18" blown glass vase shapes with applied decorations, loops, rosettes, and often topped with a finial such as a rooster. Most of these ornate banks were made as gifts or presentation pieces by the glass blowers for family or friends. Many of the glass banks contain a coin molded in the glass which helps date the piece. The earliest known glass bank with a coin is dated 1831.

McKee and Brothers of Pittsburgh list in their 1887 catalog two pressed glass banks — a dome bank and a cabinet bank. The dome bank is a building with stars in the ceiling, raised slot, and a tin screw-on bottom. Today we know this bank as the Planetarium. The cabinet bank is a house with raised center chimney slot and slide-on tin bottom.

At the turn of the century glass manufacturers began turning out pieces that could serve two purposes. They were sold with candy, condiments, syrup, or drink mixes, and when empty could be used as a bank. Most were figural glass with tin lids.

The first candy container banks appeared about 1912 – 1915. Many of these banks were figures standing next to a barrel-shaped container that held the candy. When the candy was gone the barrel with tin slotted lid became a glass bank.

The bottle banks holding condiments, syrups, and drink mixes first appeared in the 1930s. Most of these were figural bottles with tin or plastic slotted lids. If the lid was not slotted it was usually marked to have a slot punched when empty. Today manufacturers in the U.S. and, or Canada occasionally produce a new figural glass bank, usually containing peanut butter as the point of sale product.

All glass banks, such as the pigs, globes, etc., have been produced since the turn of the century and continue to be made today periodically. Bottle and window glasshouses, especially in South Jersey were known to make a number of blown bottle glass banks. Today there are flask banks still being hand blown at New Jersey's Clevenger Brothers Factory.

Glass Bank Categories

Glass Bottle Banks:
GB   Bottles with label and contents
           Bottles missing label and contents
           Bottles that never had contents
KIGB   Kraft Food & CPC International
BBGB Baby Bottle Banks
MBGB Milk Bottle Banks
ABGB Alcohol Bottle Banks
GSGB Giant Size Bottle Banks
AMGB Artist Made Glass Banks
           Folk Art Painted Banks

Inverted Bottle Banks:
IGB   Bottles with lids on the bottom
UD   Bottles with bottom lids that will stand up if inverted

All Glass Banks:
AG   All machine molded glass banks
           Banks hand blown into a mold

Flasks:
FL   Raised slot coin flask bank
FLB   Bottle neck flask with side coin slot

Combination Glass Banks:
CG   Glass banks that include metal, leather, wood, cardboard, or plastic

Blown Glass Banks:
BG   Free-blown glass banks

Fabricated Glass Banks:
FG   Glass banks created wtih leaded glass, using stained glass, clear glass, or glass with screened images

Candy Container Banks:
CC   Those accepted by the CCC of America
           Those that seem to fit this category
           Those found with slots that do not usually have slots

Glass Bubble Banks:
BB   Glass globes with a figure inside attached to a wooden base

Fish Bowl Banks:
FB   Fish bowl banks with one-piece or two-piece lids and locks

Glass Bricks or Blocks:
BL   Six sizes square: 11¾", 7¾", 5¾", 4¾", 4½", 3¼"
           Also rectangular, corner blocks, edge blocks

Advertising Mug Banks:
AM   Mug bank sizes: 5¾", 5⅜", 5¼", 5", 4⅞", 3⅜"

Milk Glass, Custard Glass, Opal Glass, Vaseline Glass Banks:
These are identified in the bank descriptions or listed as variations.

Bank Slots

Bottle Banks

Punched – Coin slot is factory punched or molded at the time of production.

Punched and Non-slotted – The bottle comes from the factory both ways.

Marked Slot – Bottle lid is marked to have a slot punched after purchase.

Questionable – Not sure if slot is authentic from the factory.

Converted Slot – Slot was punched by machine or hand after production and purchase.

All Glass Banks

Raised Slot – Slot is molded in production in a raised form.

Raised Round Slot – Slot is formed in a raised round area on top of the bank.

Molded Slot – Slot is molded or stretched at time of production.

Punch Out Slot – A pre-molded thin spot in the bank to be punched out by the bank owner.

Cut Slot – Slot cut by diamond saw at the time of production.

Large Oval Slot – Used in glass blocks to create a change holder that allows easy removal of the coins without breaking the block. Also used in the bottom as a trap hole.

Measurements

All of the banks are measured by their height, from table top to top of bank with the lid on if it is a bottle bank. A few long horizontal banks have their length given also as a measurement.

Measurements are to the nearest ¹⁄₁₆". Variations exist.

Rating, Grading

As with any collectible, rating and grading are quite difficult. There are always some avid collectors that are willing to pay much more for a bank than most average collectors. This should not necessarily set the price, but this along with rarity tends to set each bank into a price category or range. When the top collectors all have a certain bank the price usually drops, however, with the Internet, new collectors seem to be raising the prices, rather than dropping them.

Each bank shown is given a rating which includes a price range that the bank has fallen into when sold at shows, by dealers on the Internet, in private sales, or by auction.

Bottle banks that have a label that is still intact and in good condition and contents will have a much greater value.

Chips in glass banks can reduce value by half. Cracks in glass banks almost eliminate any value, unless they are quite rare. If the bank is rare and cracked, it may still be worth ¼ to ½ of the perfect condition value. Roughness or very minor chipping on cut or ground edges (such as coin slots on bubble banks) does not greatly affect value.

The banks are rated A (most common, least expensive) to very rare (price is negotiable, value is well over $1,000.00).

Uncle Sam bubble bank page 209

A	To $15.00
B	$15.00 – 35.00
C	$35.00 – 75.00
D	$75.00 – 150.00
E	$150.00 – 300.00
F	$300.00 – 600.00
Rare	$600.00 – 1,000.00
Very Rare	negotiable

Collecting Today & Tomorrow

There are still many glass banks that are common and easy to find at flea markets, yard sales, and antique shows. The Snow Crest bear in the medium size is still perhaps the most common glass bottle bank. Snow Crest also made some very rare glass banks including the clown bust, seal, and penguin. In all glass banks, the carnival pigs, both large and small, are perhaps the most common and easy to find. The carnival glass rabbits, which look similar to the pigs, are quite hard to find and bring 10 to 20 times the price of the pigs.

Up until recently, the set of galaxy spacemen (10), were difficult to find and brought as much as $150.00 each. Recently a whole warehouse of these empty bottles with boxes and separate lables were discovered and many collectors, thinking they were getting a bargain, paid a premium price for a set in the box. Today there are so many for sale the price has dropped to $5.00 – $10.00 each.

All of the glass banks that still have original paper labels of any type, such as bottles with content lables, war bond labels, or "How to Break Open" labels will always bring a higher price than the same bank without the label. The content label will always determine a much greater price difference.

Taiwan importers from time to time produce glass banks that are new, not copies of old banks. Many times these are one time, one shot productions. A serious collector would buy any of these glass banks that came on the market.

The Glass Bank Collector Newsletter
Information on collecting glass banks
Published three times a year.
Brian Cleary, Editor
P.O. Box 155
Poland, NY 13431

Future Updates to this Work
The author owns the majority of the banks represented in the book and has been a collector of glass banks since the 1960s. If you have any glass bank not shown in this book or any on his want list, please contact Charlie Reynolds. If your bank is not for sale, a photo and information would be appreciated. Thanks.
Charlie Reynolds
2836 Monroe Street
Falls Church, VA 22042-2007
Ph: (703) 533-1322
e-mail: reynoldstoys@erols.com
website: reynoldstoys.com

✗ ✓ I have these banks!

Bottle Banks

No.: GB-1
NAME: Snow Crest Bear
HEIGHT: 8½"
SLOT: punched
INFO: large; Lid — Snow Crest bank and refrigerator bottle
GRADE: C

✓ No.: GB-2 ✗
NAME: Snow Crest Bear
HEIGHT: 7⅛"
SLOT: punched
INFO: medium; Lid — Snow Crest bank bottle; Bottom — Patent Pend MFRD by Snow Crest Beverages Inc., Salem, Mass.
GRADE: C

Paid $2.⁰⁰

No.: GB-3
NAME: Snow Crest Bear
HEIGHT: 4¾"
SLOT: non-slotted
INFO: small; Lid — plain white or red and white with shaker holes
GRADE: C

No.: GB-4
NAME: Snow Crest Seal
HEIGHT: 7⅜"
SLOT: punched
INFO: Bottom — Patent Pend MFRD by Snow Crest Beverages Inc., Salem, Mass.
GRADE: F

No.: GB-5
NAME: Snow Crest Clown
HEIGHT: 7⅛"
SLOT: punched
INFO: Bottom — Patent Pend MFRD by Snow Crest Beverages Inc., Salem, Mass.
GRADE: F

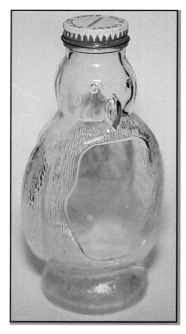

NO.:   GB-6
NAME: Snow Crest Penguin
HEIGHT: 7½"
SLOT: punched
INFO: Bottom — Patent Pend
MFRD by Snow Crest Beverages Inc., Salem, Mass.
GRADE: F

NO.:   GB-7
NAME: Snow Crest Bear
HEIGHT: 7⅛"
SLOT: punched
INFO: amber; Bottom —
Patent Pend MFRD by Snow
Crest Beverages Inc., Salem,
Mass.
GRADE: E

NO.:   GB-8
NAME: Snow Crest
HEIGHT: 7⅛"
SLOT: punched
INFO: 16 oz.; Lid — Snow
Crest bottle bank
GRADE: C

RATING, GRADING	
A	To $15.00
B	$15.00 – 35.00
C	$35.00 – 75.00
D	$75.00 – 150.00
E	$150.00 – 300.00
F	$300.00 – 600.00
Rare	$600.00 – 1,000.00
Very Rare	negotiable

NO.:   GB-9
NAME: Snow Crest
HEIGHT: 7⅛"
SLOT: punched
INFO: 16 oz; Lid — Snow
Crest bottle bank; Flavor
Labels — Orange, Cherry,
Grape
GRADE: D

NO.:   GB-10
NAME: Early Grapette Elephant
HEIGHT: 7³⁄₁₆"
SLOT: punched
INFO: square eyes, flat ears; Lid
— Grapette Family Beverage,
Syrup, Clown Head; Bottom —
Grapette Products Co., Camden,
Ark.
GRADE: Rare

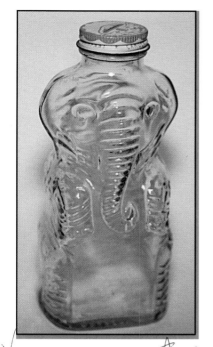

No.: GB-11
NAME: Grapette Elephant
HEIGHT: 7³⁄₁₆"
SLOT: punched
INFO: Lid — Grapette Family Beverage, Syrup, Clown Head; bottom — Grapette Products Co., Camden, Ark.
GRADE: C

paid #4

No.: GB-12
NAME: Grapette Clown
HEIGHT: 7⅛"
SLOT: punched
INFO: Lid — Grapette Family Beverage, Syrup, Clown Head; bottom — Grapette Products Co., Camden, Ark.
GRADE: B

paid 4.00

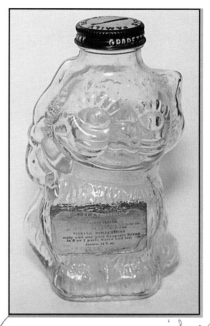

No.: GB-13
NAME: Grapette Cat
HEIGHT: 6¾"
SLOT: punched
INFO: Lid — Family Beverage Syrup; Bottom — Hammans Beverages, Springfield, Ohio
GRADE: C

paid #4.

No.: GB-14
NAME: Grapette
HEIGHT: 11⅝"
SLOT: punched
INFO: gallon; Grapette Family Beverage, Syrup, Clown Head; Label — Root Beer
GRADE: E

No.: GB-15
NAME: Louisiana Vinegar Clown
HEIGHT: 7⅛"
SLOT: punched
INFO: Lid — Grapette Family Beverage, Syrup, Clown Head; Bottom — Grapette Products Co., Camden, Ark.
GRADE: C

NO.: GB-16
NAME: Cat
HEIGHT: 6¾"
SLOT: punched
INFO: Lid — plain white; Bottom — Glass Mold Numbers; bought in gift shop as a bank
GRADE: C

NO.: GB-17
NAME: Clown
HEIGHT: 7⅛"
SLOT: punched
INFO: Lid — plain white; Bottom — Grapette Ball MFG.
GRADE: C

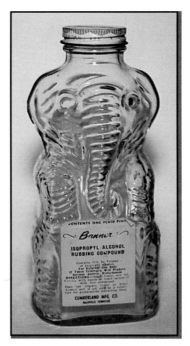

NO.: GB-18
NAME: Banner Alcohol Elephant
HEIGHT: 7³⁄₁₆"
SLOT: punched
INFO: Lid — Grapette Family Beverage, Syrup, Clown Head; Bottom — Grapette Products Co., Camden, Ark.
GRADE: C

NO.: GB-19
NAME: Lincoln bottle
HEIGHT: 9⅞"
SLOT: punched
INFO: Lid — plain black short; Bottom — Lincoln Foods, Lawrence, Mass.
GRADE: B

NO.: GB-20
NAME: Lincoln bottle
HEIGHT: 8½"
SLOT: punched
INFO: Lid — Lincoln Bank Bottle, picture of Lincoln, tall, top threads; rare labels
GRADE: D

NO.: GB-21
NAME: Lincoln bottle
HEIGHT: 8½"
SLOT: punched
INFO: Lid — Lincoln bank bottle, picture of Lincoln, tall, top threads
GRADE: C

NO.: GB-22
NAME: Lincoln bottle
HEIGHT: 9¾"
SLOT: punched
INFO: Lid — Lincoln Bank Bottle, picture of Lincoln, tall, all threaded
GRADE: B

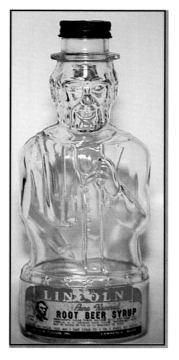

NO.: GB-23
NAME: Lincoln bottle
HEIGHT: 8½"
SLOT: punched
INFO: Lid — plain black short
GRADE: C

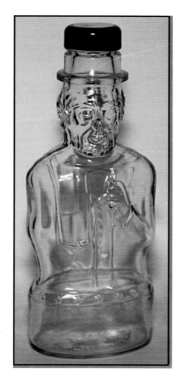

NO.: GB-24
NAME: Lincoln bottle
HEIGHT: 8⅞"
SLOT: marked slot
INFO: Lid — ketchup twist-off type, black, white, short
GRADE: B

See page 7 for price ranges.

NO.: GB-25
NAME: Yankee Witch Hazel, Lincoln bottle
HEIGHT: 8⅞"
SLOT: marked slot
INFO: Lid — ketchup twist-off type, black, white, tall
GRADE: D

NO.: GB-26
NAME: For Your Lincoln Pen-
nies, Lincoln bottle
HEIGHT: 8⅞"
SLOT: marked slot
INFO: Lid — ketchup twist-
off type, black, white, tall
GRADE: D

NO.: GB-27
NAME: SAVE Wayside Indus-
tries, Lincoln bottle
HEIGHT: 8⅞"
SLOT: marked slot
INFO: Lid — ketchup twist-off
type, black, white, short
GRADE: D

NO.: GB-28
NAME: Lincoln Bottle,
1984, I.E.F.P.,
Washington, D.C.
Height: 7¾"
Slot: non-slotted
Info: Lid — black plastic;
Front bottom — Container
General Corp.
Grade: D

NO.: GB-29
NAME: Administration Building
HEIGHT: 3¼"
SLOT: punched
INFO: Lid — gold, black, six stars
embossed, also Roman head with
laurel wreath and star
GRADE: E

RATING, GRADING	
A	To $15.00
B	$15.00 – 35.00
C	$35.00 – 75.00
D	$75.00 – 150.00
E	$150.00 – 300.00
F	$300.00 – 600.00
Rare	$600.00 – 1,000.00
Very Rare	negotiable

NO.: GB-30
Name: Uncle Sam Bond
Height: 9¼"
Slot: punched
Info: Lid — plain black, short;
Back — Cut Your Beverage Cost,
Save and Buy War Bonds, This Is
Your Bond Bank, Uncle Sam Syrup
Co., Rochester, N.Y., 16 oz.
Grade: F

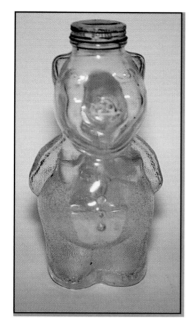

NO.: GB-31
NAME: Fred Fear Pig
HEIGHT: 7¾"
SLOT: punched
INFO: large; Lid — Piggy Bank Bottle; has fur design on front of legs
GRADE: C

NO.: GB-32
NAME: Fred Fear Pig
HEIGHT: 7¾"
SLOT: punched
INFO: large; Lid — New England Syrup, Piggy Bank Bottle; no fur design on front of legs
GRADE: C

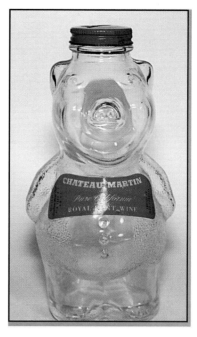

NO.: GB-33
NAME: Chateau Martin Wine Pig
HEIGHT: 7¾"
SLOT: punched
INFO: large; Lid — plain red; no fur design on front of legs
GRADE: D

NO.: GB-34
NAME: Fred Fear Pig
HEIGHT: 7⅛"
SLOT: punched
INFO: small; Lid — New England Syrup; three buttons pushed out on front, palm out in back
GRADE: B

NO.: GB-35
NAME: Fred Fear Pig
Height: 7⅛"
SLOT: punched
INFO: small; Lid — New England Syrup; three buttons pushed in on front, palm in on back
GRADE: B

No.: GB-36
NAME: Porky Pinx
HEIGHT: 7¹³⁄₁₆"
SLOT: punched
INFO: Lid — white with pink plastic hat; three buttons pushed in on front, palm in on back; also found in mint green with white lid, ribbon and bow around neck
GRADE: D

No.: GB-37
NAME: Forbes Piggy
HEIGHT: 4¼"
SLOT: punched
INFO: Lid — Prepared Mustard, Jas. H. Forbes, Tea & Coffee Co., St. Louis, Mo., 6 oz.
GRADE: C

No.: GB-38
NAME: Gedney's Piggy
HEIGHT: 4¼"
SLOT: punched
INFO: mustard; Lid — M.A. Gedney Co., Minneapolis, Minn., 7 oz. AVD
GRADE: C

No.: GB-39
NAME: Little Pig
HEIGHT: 4¼"
SLOT: punched
INFO: mustard; Lid — Western Food Prod. Co., Hutchinson, Kansas, 6 oz.; also Bailey Manufacturing Co., Oklahoma City, OK, variation
GRADE: C

No.: GB-40
NAME: Piggy, "Nutty Club"
HEIGHT: 4¼"
SLOT: punched
INFO: Peanut butter; Lid — Scott-Bathgate Ltd., Winnipeg & Vancouver, 6 oz. Net
GRADE: D

No.: GB-41
NAME: Piggy,
HEIGHT: 4¼"
SLOT: punched
INFO: Lid — Piggy Bank, U.S. Coffee & Tea Co., Dallas
GRADE: D

NO.: GB-42
NAME: Brother Can You
Spare a Dime? Pig
HEIGHT: 5⅛"
SLOT: punched
INFO: Lid — red, gold
with name; comes with several different labels and
manufacturers
GRADE: B

NO.: GB-43
NAME: Jocko Monkey
HEIGHT: 5"
SLOT: punched
INFO: Lid — red, gold, Prepared Mustard, Jocko picture
of monkey, 8½ oz.; The
Newton Products Co., Cincinnati, Ohio, Atlanta, GA
GRADE: E

RATING, GRADING	
A	To $15.00
B	$15.00 – 35.00
C	$35.00 – 75.00
D	$75.00 – 150.00
E	$150.00 – 300.00
F	$300.00 – 600.00
Rare	$600.00 – 1,000.00
Very Rare	negotiable

NO.: GB-44
NAME: Log Cabin
HEIGHT: 4¾"
SLOT: punched
INFO: Lid — red, white; Log Cabin name on
roof; Log Cabin Syrup
GRADE: B

NO.: GB-45
NAME: Log Cabin, no name
HEIGHT: 4¾"
SLOT: punched
INFO: Lid — red, white; no name on roof; Log
Cabin Syrup
GRADE: C

NO.: GB-46
NAME: Gattuso Pig in Sailor Suit
HEIGHT: 6¼"
SLOT: punched
INFO: Lid — yellow, red, blue, silver, Gattuso Bambino Olives, picture of baby; painted by owner
GRADE: B

NO.: GB-47
NAME: Gattuso Pig in Sailor Suit
HEIGHT: 6¼"
SLOT: punched
INFO: 16 oz.; Lid — yellow, red, blue, white, Gattuso Bambino Olives, no baby
GRADE: C

NO.: GB-48
NAME: Gattuso Rabbit
HEIGHT: 6⅜"
SLOT: punched
INFO: Lid — yellow, red, blue, white, Gattuso Bambino Olives, no baby
GRADE: F

NO.: GB-49
NAME: Gattuso Rabbit
HEIGHT: 6⅜"
SLOT: punched
INFO: 16 oz.; Lid — yellow, red, blue, white, Gattuso Bambino Olives, no baby
GRADE: F

NO.: GB-50
NAME: Gattuso Owl
HEIGHT: 6¾"
SLOT: punched
INFO: Lid — yellow, red, blue, white, Gattuso Bambino Olives, picture of baby
GRADE: C

NO.: GB-51
NAME: Diamant Pig
HEIGHT: 9⅜"
SLOT: punched
INFO: Lid — picture of hand putting coin in slot; picture of sparkling diamond, Enjoy all Diamond Brands For Health Then Use This Bank for Thrift and Wealth; Ste-Marie CTE Beauce P. Q.
GRADE: E

NO.: GB-52
NAME: Penguin Bubble Gum
HEIGHT: 8"
SLOT: punched & non-slotted
INFO: Lid — plain white; used by several companies and products
GRADE: C

RATING, GRADING	
A	To $15.00
B	$15.00 – 35.00
C	$35.00 – 75.00
D	$75.00 – 150.00
E	$150.00 – 300.00
F	$300.00 – 600.00
Rare	$600.00 – 1,000.00
Very Rare	negotiable

NO.: GB-53
NAME: Lucky Jumbo
HEIGHT: 7"
SLOT: punched
INFO: wide; Lid — Lucky Jumbo Bank; Bottom — Castle Products, Newark, N.J., Pat. Applied For
GRADE: B

NO.: GB-54
NAME: Lucky Jumbo
HEIGHT: 7⅛"
SLOT: punched
INFO: thin; Lid — Lucky Jumbo Bank; Bottom — Castle Products, Newark, N.J., USA
GRADE: C

NO.: GB-55
NAME: Earliest Lucky Joe
HEIGHT: 4½"
SLOT: punched
INFO: Lid — Nash's Prepared Mustard, Nash-Underwood Inc., Chicago, ILL, 8½ oz.; Label — paper face with square corners; Bottom — Ball Glass
GRADE: D

NO.: GB-56
NAME: Early Lucky Joe
HEIGHT: 4½"
SLOT: punched
INFO: Lid — Nash's Prepared Mustard, Nash-Underwood Inc., Chicago, ILL, 8½ oz.; Label — paper face with round corners; Bottom — Ball Glass
GRADE: D

NO.: GB-57
NAME: Lucky Joe
HEIGHT: 4⁹⁄₁₆"
SLOT: punched
INFO: Lid — Nash's Prepared Mustard, Nash-Underwood Inc., Chicago, ILL, 8½ oz.; Label — paper lips; Bottom — Design Patent No. 112688
GRADE: B

RATING, GRADING	
A	To $15.00
B	$15.00 – 35.00
C	$35.00 – 75.00
D	$75.00 – 150.00
E	$150.00 – 300.00
F	$300.00 – 600.00
Rare	$600.00 – 1,000.00
Very Rare	negotiable

NO.: GB-58
NAME: Jolly Joe
HEIGHT: 4⁹⁄₁₆"
SLOT: punched
INFO: Lid — Nash's Prepared Mustard, Nash-Underwood Inc., Chicago, 8½ oz.; Label — paper lips; Bottom — Design Patent No. 112688
GRADE: C

NO.: GB-59
NAME: Quality Prepared Mustard, Face Lid
HEIGHT: 4⁹⁄₁₆"
SLOT: punched
INFO: Lid — Save Your Money, face with mouth slot; Label — paper lips with Nash-Underwood, Inc., Chicago, Ill.
GRADE: D

NO.: GB-60
NAME: Deerwood
HEIGHT: 4⁹⁄₁₆"
SLOT: punched
INFO: Lid — Save At Deerwood Bank, UBC Distributors, Chicago, Ill, San Francisco, Calif., Prepared Mustard, 8½ oz.
GRADE: D

NO.: GB-61
NAME: Royal Blue
HEIGHT: 4⁹⁄₁₆"
SLOT: punched
INFO: Lid — Save At Royal Blue Bank, Royal Blue Stores Inc. Distributors, Chicago, Ill, Prepared Mustard, 8½ oz.
GRADE: D

NO.: GB-62
NAME: Centrella Foods
HEIGHT: 4⁹⁄₁₆"
SLOT: punched
INFO: Lid — Centrella Foods Bank, Packed For Central Grocers Co-Op, Inc., Chicago, Ill.
GRADE: D

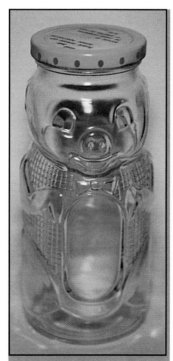
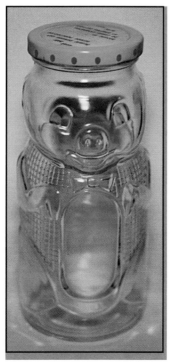

NO.: GB-63
NAME: Coronation Pig
HEIGHT: 7½"
SLOT: punched
INFO: Lid — Dear Dad! Please Remove Cap Before Punching, also same instruction in French
GRADE: C

NO.: GB-64
NAME: Domino Sugar Bear
HEIGHT: 4½"
SLOT: molded in plastic under lid
INFO: Lid — red, yellow, Mr. Bear's a Bank, Too!; Label — Domino Sugar 'n Cinnamon, 3¼ oz.; Back — American Sugar Refining Co., N.Y., N.Y.
GRADE: B

NO.: GB-65
NAME: Sunny Cane Bear
HEIGHT: 4½"
SLOT: molded in plastic under lid
INFO: Lid — blue, yellow, Mr. Bear's a Bank, Too!; Label — Sunny Cane Sugar 'n Cinnamon, 3¼ oz.; Back — McCahan Sugar Refinery, Phila.
GRADE: B

NO.: GB-66
NAME: Sunny Cane Sun Label Bear
HEIGHT: 4½"
SLOT: molded in plastic under lid
INFO: Lid — blue, yellow, Mr. Bear's a Bank, Too!; Label — Sunny Cane in Sun label; Back — McCahan Sugar Refinery, Phila.
GRADE: B

NO.: GB-67
NAME: Franklin Sugar Bear
HEIGHT: 4½"
SLOT: molded in plastic under lid
INFO: Lid — blue, white, Mr. Bear's a Bank, Too!; Label — Franklin Sugar 'n Cinnamon, 3¼ oz.; Back — Franklin Sugar Refinery
GRADE: B

NO.: GB-68
NAME: Spreckels Bear
HEIGHT: 4½"
SLOT: molded plastic under lid
INFO: Lid — white, Mr. Bear's a Bank, Too!; Label — Spreckels Sugar & Cinnamon, 3¼ oz; Back — Spreckels Sugar Co., San Francisco
GRADE: C

NO.: GB-69
NAME: Carnival Glass Sugar Bear
HEIGHT: 4½"
SLOT: molded in plastic under lid
INFO: Lid — white, Mr. Bear's a Bank, Too!
GRADE: D

NO.: GB-70
NAME: Nash Liberty Bell
HEIGHT: 3¾"
SLOT: punched and non-slotted
INFO: Lid — red, white, blue, Liberty Bell, Nash's Mustard, Nash Underwood, Chicago, 8½ oz.
GRADE: B

No.: GB-71
NAME: Man in Striped Pants
HEIGHT: 5"
SLOT: non-slotted
INFO: Lid — green or blue, Premium Prepared Mustard with Horseradish; Bottom — Plochman & Harrison, Chicago, Pat. Pend.
GRADE: C

No.: GB-72
NAME: Nash Liberty Bell
HEIGHT: 5⅝"
SLOT: punched
INFO: tall, ribbed; Lid — red, white, blue, Liberty Bell, Nash's Mustard, Nash Underwood, Chicago, 8½ oz.
GRADE: C

No.: GB-73
NAME: Donald Duck
HEIGHT: 4½"
SLOT: punched
INFO: Lid — blue, yellow, Donald Duck Bank, Nash Quality Mustard; Label — comes with eye and beak, paper label (see Glass Banks with Rare Labels section)
GRADE: C

No.: GB-74
NAME: Donald Duck
HEIGHT: 4½"
SLOT: punched
INFO: Lid — red, white, Nash Try Our Tic Tic Relish, Kiddy Bank, Prepared Mustard, Nash-Underwood Inc., Chicago
GRADE: C

No.: GB-75
NAME: Donald Duck
HEIGHT: 4½"
SLOT: punched
INFO: Lid — blue, yellow, Nash Quality, Try Donald Duck Peanut Butter; Bottom Edge — Donald Duck in raised letters, both sides; name in glass
GRADE: C

No.: GB-76
NAME: Donald Duck
HEIGHT: 4½"
SLOT: punched
INFO: Lid — red, yellow, Nash Quality Products
GRADE: C

No.: GB-77
NAME: Donald Duck
HEIGHT: 4½"
SLOT: non-slotted
INFO: Lid — blue, yellow, Donald Duck Suggests You Try Nash's Quality Peanut Butter
GRADE: D

No.: GB-78
NAME: Deerwood Donald Duck
HEIGHT: 4½"
SLOT: punched
INFO: Lid — blue, white, Save at Deerwood Bank, Distributed by UBC Dist., Chicago, San Francisco, CA, Prepared Mustard, 8½ oz.
GRADE: D

No.: GB-79
NAME: Lucky Joe Donald Duck
HEIGHT: 4½"
SLOT: punched
INFO: Lid — red, white, Nash's Prepared Mustard, Lucky Joe Bank, Nash-Underwood, Inc., Chicago, 8½ oz.
GRADE: C

See page 7 for price ranges.

No.: GB-80
NAME: Royal Blue Donald Duck
HEIGHT: 4½"
SLOT: punched
INFO: Lid — blue, white, Save at Royal Blue Bank, Royal Blue Stores Inc., Distribution Chicago, Ill., Prepared Mustard, 8½ oz.
GRADE: D

No.: GB-81
NAME: Donald Duck
HEIGHT: 4$^{15}/_{16}$"
SLOT: punched
INFO: round; Lid — blue, yellow; Label — Donald Duck Relish
GRADE: D

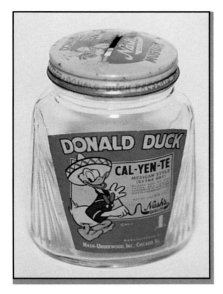

NO.: GB-82
NAME: Donald Duck Cal-Yen-Te
HEIGHT: 4"
SLOT: punched
INFO: Lid — red, yellow, Donald Duck Bank, Nash Quality Mustard; Label — Donald Duck Cal-Yen-Te, Mexican Style Extra Hot, Nash-Underwood Inc., Chicago, ILL, 8½ oz.
GRADE: D

NO.: GB-83
NAME: Donald Duck
HEIGHT: 4⅛"
SLOT: punched
INFO: wide ribbed; Lid — blue, yellow, Donald Duck Bank, Nash Quality Mustard; Label — Donald Duck Prepared Mustard, Golden Cream, Nash-Underwood Inc., Chicago, Ill., 8½ oz.
GRADE: D

NO.: GB-84
NAME: Donald Duck Rusty Label
HEIGHT: 4⅛"
SLOT: punched
INFO: Lid — red, yellow; Label — Rusty and Rin Tin Tin, not sure if original or a premium you sent for to add to your bank
GRADE: C

NO.: GB-85
NAME: Tilting Man with Monocle
HEIGHT: 4⅜"
SLOT: non-slotted
INFO: Lid — red, gold, Sun-Ra Hot Dog Sauce, Sun-Ra Products Co., St. Joseph, MO, 8 oz.; Label on back — hot dog shape, Hot Dog Sauce (lists uses)
GRADE: C

NO.: GB-86
NAME: Tilting Man Winking
HEIGHT: 4⅜"
SLOT: non-slotted
INFO: Lid — red, gold, Sun-Ra Hot Dog Sauce, Su-Ra Products Co., St., Joseph, MO, 8 oz.
GRADE: C

NO.: GB-87
NAME: Tilting Man Frowning
HEIGHT: 4⅜"
SLOT: non-slotted
INFO: Lid — red, gold, Sun-Ra Hot Dog Sauce, Sun-Ra Products Co., St. Joseph, MO, 8 oz.
GRADE: C

No.: GB-88
Name: Tilting Man Smiling
Height: 4⅜"
Slot: non-slotted
Info: Lid — red, gold, Sun-Ra Hot Dog Sauce, Sun-Ra Products Co., St. Joseph, MO, 8 oz.
Grade: C

No.: GB-89
Name: Tilting Man with Monocle
Height: 4⅜"
Slot: non-slotted
Info: amber; Lid — red, gold, Sun-Ra Hot Dog Sauce, Sun-Ra Products Co., St. Joseph, MO, 8 oz.
Grade: D

No.: GB-90
Name: Two Faced Fox
Height: 8¾"
Slot: punched
Info: Lid — red, white, Easy Pour Drink Guide, Enjoy the Many Other U-Bet Flavors (variation large letters); Label — U-Bet Pure Fruit Flavor Syrup, H. Fox & Co. Inc., Brooklyn, N.Y., 12 oz.
Grade: C

No.: GB-91
Name: Bosco Clown with label (rare)
Height: 7¾"
Slot: marked punch out slot
Info: Lid — brown, gold tin (shown in next row); Label — rare with wrap around label, Best Foods, Division Corn Products Co., New York, N.Y.
Grade: E (without label — Grade B)

Bosco Clown showing label on lid.

NO.: GB-92
NAME: Bosco Bear
HEIGHT: 7½"
SLOT: marked punch out slot
INFO: large; Lid — usually missing metal lid; Bottom — Bosco name in cross pattern
GRADE: B

NO.: GB-93
NAME: Bosco Bear
HEIGHT: 7¼"
SLOT: marked punch out slot
INFO: small; Lid — usually missing metal lid; Bottom — Bosco name in cross pattern
GRADE: C

NO.: GB-94
NAME: Bosco Clown
HEIGHT: 7¾"
SLOT: non-slotted
INFO: Lid — red, white, Bosco on Ice Cream; Bottom — Bosco name in cross pattern
GRADE: D

NO.: GB-95
NAME: Tankar System Saves
HEIGHT: 3¾"
SLOT: punched
INFO: Lid — plain white; Tankar System Saves on both sides of bank
GRADE: D (rare with celluloid collar on lid)

No.: GB-96
NAME: Playtown Budget
HEIGHT: 1 1/16"
SLOT: punched
INFO: Lid — red, gold, white, Gold Medal Playtown, You'll Have Sense If You Save, Budget Bank, Transogram Co. Inc. N.Y. (comes in Playtown Banker game by Transogram 1940s)
GRADE: B

No.: GB-97
NAME: Baby Cream
HEIGHT: 1"
SLOT: punched and non-slotted
INFO: Lid — maroon, white, gold, gold medal doctor & nurse, jar for baby cream, Copyright MCMXLV Transogram Co. N.Y. (comes in doctor and nurse kits by Transogram 1940s)
GRADE: E

No.: GB-98
NAME: Early Liberty Cherries
HEIGHT: 3½"
SLOT: non-slotted
INFO: Lid — blue, silver, Liberty Cherries, picture of Statue of Liberty; Label — thin paper label; Liberty Cherries and molded crack in glass
GRADE: B

RATING, GRADING	
A	To $15.00
B	$15.00 – 35.00
C	$35.00 – 75.00
D	$75.00 – 150.00
E	$150.00 – 300.00
F	$300.00 – 600.00
Rare	$600.00 – 1,000.00
Very Rare	negotiable

No.: GB-99
NAME: Liberty Cherries
HEIGHT: 3⅜"
SLOT: non-slotted
INFO: Lid — red, white, blue, Liberty Maraschino Cherries, Net. Wt. 6 oz.; Liberty 1776 – 1976 and molded crack in glass
GRADE: A

No.: GB-100
NAME: Liberty Spanish Olives
HEIGHT: 3⅜"
SLOT: non-slotted
INFO: Lid — white, black, green, Liberty Spanish Olives, picture of Liberty Bell; Liberty 1776 – 1976 and molded crack in glass
GRADE: A

No.: GB-101
NAME: Bridgeton "Gem O' Jersey"
HEIGHT: 4¾"
SLOT: punched and non-slotted
INFO: To Commemorate the Founding of Bridgeton, N.J. 1686 – 1936
GRADE: D

No.: GB-102
NAME: Gayner Bell
HEIGHT: 6¼"
SLOT: converted
INFO: Merry Christmas, picture of Santa; Christmas Party 1941, Gayner Glass Works, Salem, N.J., Established 1879
GRADE: E

No.: GB-103
NAME: Black Banded Barrel
HEIGHT: 5½"
SLOT: lid not yet found
INFO: four molded painted barrel bands, molded wooden stays; Bottom — molded concentric circles
GRADE: C

No.: GB-104
NAME: Feed the Kitty Bucket
HEIGHT: 4¾"
SLOT: punched
INFO: Lid — white, red, blue, South Shore, Feed the Kitty Bucket bank, Spanish Olives, Net Wt. 6 oz.
GRADE: E

No.: GB-105
NAME: Handi Square
HEIGHT: 4⅞"
SLOT: questionable
INFO: Lid — red, white, blue, South Shore, Spanish Olives, picture of sail boat; framing square and word Handi Molded in glass
GRADE: C

No.: GB-106
NAME: Dailey's Barrel
HEIGHT: 4⅛"
SLOT: punched
INFO: Lid — black on white; Buy a Barrel of Pickles, Save a Barrel of Money
GRADE: D

No.: GB-107
NAME: You Can Always Bank on Pickles!
HEIGHT: 6⅛"
SLOT: punched
INFO: Lid — white, light green, You Can Always Bank On Pickles!; screened green, white pickles singing and dancing
GRADE: D

No.: GB-108
NAME: Tall Barrel
HEIGHT: 7½"
SLOT: punched
INFO: Lid — dark blue; molded six bands with wood staves
GRADE: B

No.: GB-109
NAME: Old Barrel
HEIGHT: 4"
SLOT: punched
INFO: Lid — unpainted tin; molded four banks with middle bung hole
GRADE: C

No.: GB-110
NAME: Battleship Mustard
HEIGHT: 3½"
SLOT: punched
INFO: Lid — black and gold or black and silver, Battleship Prepared Mustard, Brand Highest Quality, Packed by Wm. S. Scull Co., Dayton, Ohio, Net Wt. 5 oz
GRADE: A

NO.: GB-111
NAME: Kroger Barrel
HEIGHT: 3½"
SLOT: punched
INFO: Lid — red, white, Kroger's Country Club Quality Prepared Mustard, Net Wt. 5 oz., Distributed by the Kroger Grocery & Baking Co., Cinn., O
GRADE: B

NO.: GB-112
NAME: Koop's Tall Thin Barrel
HEIGHT: 4¾"
SLOT: punched
INFO: Lid — red, white, Koop's Mustard Barrel Bank
GRADE: B

NO.: GB-113
NAME: Koop's Barrel
HEIGHT: 4¹/₁₆"
SLOT: punched
INFO: Lid — red, white, Koop's Mustard, Barrel Bank; Label — Koop's Extra Strong Mustard, Holland Hills, Inc., Chicago 39, Ill.
GRADE: B

NO.: GB-114
NAME: Barrel
HEIGHT: 5"
SLOT: punched
INFO: Lid — gold colored tin; molded four bands with middle bung hole
GRADE: B

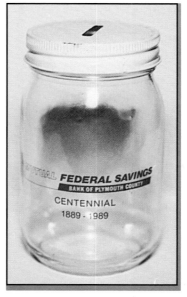

NO.: GB-115
NAME: Federal Savings Bank of Plymouth County
HEIGHT: 4¾"
SLOT: punched
INFO: Lid — plain white, Centennial 1889 – 1989
GRADE: B

31

NO.: GB 116
NAME: Dietz Jar,
       Pat. Nov. 20, 1900
HEIGHT: 4¼"
SLOT: punched
INFO: large; Lid — plain tin with pad-lock; found with Church Extension, Birthday Offering, Sunday School, Loan Fund, etched in glass
GRADE: D

NO.: GB-117
NAME: Dietz Jar,
       Pat. Nov. 20, 1900
HEIGHT: 3½"
SLOT: punched
INFO: small; Lid — plain tin with padlock
GRADE: D

NO.: GB-118
NAME: Pickle Dollar Jar
HEIGHT: 4¼"
SLOT: punched
INFO: Lid — plain white; Label — paper label inside jar
GRADE: C

See page 7 for price ranges.

NO.: GB-119
NAME: Oval Pickling Spice
HEIGHT: 4⅝"
SLOT: punched, also 10 holes
INFO: Lid — plain tin; early glass
GRADE: D

NO.: GB-120
NAME: Concave Pickling Spice
HEIGHT: 4¼"
SLOT: punched, also 10 holes
INFO: Lid — plain tin; early glass with four concave sides and starburst bottom
GRADE: C

NO.: GB-121
NAME: Ball Ten
HEIGHT: 5½"
SLOT: punched, off center
INFO: Lid — rusty; 10 molded vertical ribs, ball on bottom
GRADE: C

NO.: GB-122
NAME: Aunt Jane's
HEIGHT: 3½"
SLOT: punched, off center
INFO: Lid — repainted; rope design jar; Aunt Jane's in bottom
GRADE: C

NO.: GB-123
NAME: Wonder Bubbles
HEIGHT: 4⅜"
SLOT: punched
INFO: Lid — plain tin domed or white flat; Wonder Bubbles around top shoulder of glass
GRADE: C

NO.: GB-124
NAME: Six-sided Concave
HEIGHT: 4¹⁄₁₆"
SLOT: punched
INFO: Lid — plain white
GRADE: B

RATING, GRADING	
A	To $15.00
B	$15.00 – 35.00
C	$35.00 – 75.00
D	$75.00 – 150.00
E	$150.00 – 300.00
F	$300.00 – 600.00
Rare	$600.00 – 1,000.00
Very Rare	negotiable

NO.: GB-125
NAME: Galaxy Asteroid Commander
HEIGHT: 8½"
SLOT: punched
INFO: Lid — white, purple (grape syrup); Front and Back — pyroglazed blue, white; Bottom — Cont. 16 Fld. oz, Des. Pat Pend & Reg, Space Foods Co. Balto, MD
GRADE: A

No.: GB-126
NAME: Galaxy Space Ace
HEIGHT: 8½"
SLOT: punched
INFO: Lid — white, red (cherry syrup); Front and Back — pyroglazed red, white; Bottom — Cont. 16 Fld. oz, Des. Pat Pend & Reg, Space Foods Co. Balto, MD
GRADE: A

No.: GB-127
NAME: Galaxy Space Scout
HEIGHT: 8½"
SLOT: punched
INFO: Lid — white, purple (grape syrup); Front and Back — pyroglazed blue, white; Bottom — Cont. 16 Fld. oz, Des. Pat Pend & Reg, Space Foods Co. Balto, MD
GRADE: A

No.: GB-128
NAME: Galaxy Space Commander
HEIGHT: 8½"
SLOT: punched
INFO: Lid — white, purple (raspberry syrup); Front and Back — pyroglazed black, white; Bottom — Cont. 16 Fld. oz, Des. Pat Pend & Reg, Space Foods Co. Balto, MD
GRADE: A

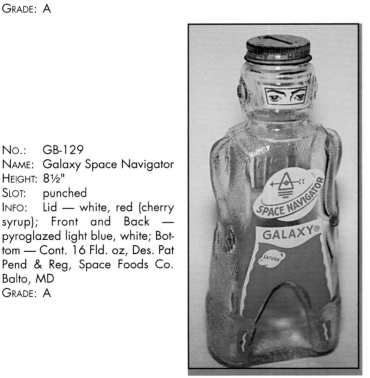

No.: GB-129
NAME: Galaxy Space Navigator
HEIGHT: 8½"
SLOT: punched
INFO: Lid — white, red (cherry syrup); Front and Back — pyroglazed light blue, white; Bottom — Cont. 16 Fld. oz, Des. Pat Pend & Reg, Space Foods Co. Balto, MD
GRADE: A

RATING, GRADING	
A	To $15.00
B	$15.00 – 35.00
C	$35.00 – 75.00
D	$75.00 – 150.00
E	$150.00 – 300.00
F	$300.00 – 600.00
Rare	$600.00 – 1,000.00
Very Rare	negotiable

NO.: GB-130
NAME: Galaxy Orbit Admiral
HEIGHT: 8½"
SLOT: punched
INFO: Lid — white, orange (orange syrup); Front and Back — pyroglazed light red, white; Bottom — Cont. 16 Fld. oz, Des. Pat Pend & Reg, Space Foods Co. Balto, MD
GRADE: A

NO.: GB-131
NAME: Galaxy Interplanetary Commander
HEIGHT: 8½"
SLOT: punched
INFO: Lid — white, orange (orange syrup); Front and Back — pyroglazed orange, white; Bottom — Cont. 16 Fld. oz, Des. Pat Pend & Reg, Space Foods Co. Balto, MD
GRADE: A

NO.: GB-132
NAME: Galaxy Space Sentry
HEIGHT: 8½"
SLOT: punched
INFO: Lid — white, red (cherry cyrup); Front and Back — pyroglazed red, white; Bottom — Cont. 16 Fld. oz, Des. Pat Pend & Reg, Space Foods Co. Balto, MD
GRADE: A

NO.: GB-133
NAME: Galaxy Space Admiral
HEIGHT: 8½"
SLOT: punched
INFO: Lid — white, red (cherry syrup); Front and Back — pyroglazed maroon, white; Bottom — Cont. 16 Fld. oz, Des. Pat Pend & Reg, Space Foods Co. Balto, MD
GRADE: A

NO.: GB-134
NAME: Galaxy Space Bombardier
HEIGHT: 8½"
SLOT: punched
INFO: Lid — white, purple (grape syrup); Front and Back — pyroglazed green, white; Bottom — Cont. 16 Fld. oz, Des. Pat Pend & Reg, Space Foods Co. Balto, MD
GRADE: A

NO.: GB-135
NAME: Kiddy Bank Tic Tic Relish
HEIGHT: 4⅜"
SLOT: punched
INFO: Lid — red, white, Kiddy Bank, Nash Try Tic Tic Relish, Prepared Mustard, Nash-Underwood Inc, Chicago; Bottom — Design Patent No. 95888
GRADE: C

NO.: GB-136
NAME: Happy Time Dutch Lunch Sauce
HEIGHT: 4¾"
SLOT: non-slotted
INFO: Lid — domed tin; Bottom — Design Patent No. 95888
GRADE: C

NO.: GB-137
NAME: Tic Tic Relish
HEIGHT: 4⅝"
SLOT: non-slotted
INFO: no clock hands; Lid — domed tin; Bottom — Design Patent No. 95888
GRADE: D

NO.: GB-138
NAME: Happy Time Horseradish Style Mustard
HEIGHT: 4⅞"
SLOT: non-slotted
INFO: Lid — domed tin; Bottom — Design Patent No. 95888
GRADE: C

NO.: GB-139
NAME: Little Elf Peanut Butter
HEIGHT: 4¾"
SLOT: non-slotted
INFO: Lid — domed tin; Bottom — Design Patent No. 95888
GRADE: D

NO.: GB-140
NAME: Small Clock (rare)
HEIGHT: 3⅝"
SLOT: non-slotted
INFO: Lid — small domed tin; Bottom — Des. Pat 95888
GRADE: E

No.: GB-141
Name: Old Fashioned Stove
Height: 5¹³⁄₁₆"
Slot: punched
Info: Lid — black or metallic red; Label — Fire Burning Inside; Other — Collectors Item, Old Fashion Stove, Assorted Sparkle, Artificially Flavored Net Wt. 8 ozs., Fresh Pak Candy Co., Moline, ILL
Grade: B

No.: GB-142
Name: Raccoon Mountain Syrup
Height: 5¹³⁄₁₆"
Slot: paper over punched slot
Info: Lid — Raccoon Mountain Syrup, Open Kettle Process, Made On Our Farm, Raccoon Mt. Sorghum Co, Pisgah, AL, Net. Wt. 20 ozs.
Grade: C

RATING, GRADING	
A	To $15.00
B	$15.00 – 35.00
C	$35.00 – 75.00
D	$75.00 – 150.00
E	$150.00 – 300.00
F	$300.00 – 600.00
Rare	$600.00 – 1,000.00
Very Rare	negotiable

No.: GB-143
Name: World's Fair Savings bank, St. Louis 1904
Height: 2½"
Slot: punched
Info: Lid — embossed aluminum
Grade: E

No.: GB-144
Name: Children's Savings bank
Height: 2½"
Slot: punched
Info: Lid — embossed aluminum
Grade: D

No.: GB-145
Name: Children's Savings bank, Old Block House 1754, Pittsburgh, PA
Height: 2½"
Slot: punched
Info: Lid — embossed aluminum
Grade: D

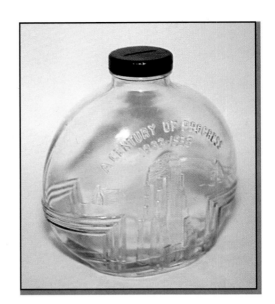

No.: GB-146
NAME: Save With Us Credit Union
HEIGHT: 5¼"
SLOT: punched
INFO: Lid — two piece brass; Save
With Us. . . Brockway Zane Federal
Credit Union
GRADE: C

No.: GB-147
NAME: Queen-O
HEIGHT: 7¼"
SLOT: punched
INFO: Lid — white; Label —
Cherry Flavor
GRADE: C

No.: GB-148
NAME: A Century of Progress, 1833 – 1933
HEIGHT: 6¼"
SLOT: converted?
INFO: Lid — black tin
GRADE: C

No.: GB-149
NAME: Green Lantern Jar
HEIGHT: 5¾"
SLOT: punched
INFO: Lid — green; dark
green glass
GRADE: D

No.: GB-150
NAME: Honey Jar with Bee
HEIGHT: 4½"
SLOT: punched
INFO: Lid — white with inner
liner, conversion?
GRADE: C

No.: GB-151
NAME: World Globe Jar
HEIGHT: 5⅜"
SLOT: punched
INFO: Lid — white, loose fit, conver-
sion?; raised continents in glass; Bottom
— Patent Applied For
GRADE: C

No.: GB-152
NAME: Burma-Shave
HEIGHT: 2¼"
SLOT: punched
INFO: Lid — No Brush – No
Lather
GRADE: C

No.: GB-153
NAME: Burma-Shave
HEIGHT: 2¼"
SLOT: punched
INFO: Lid — Burma-Vita Co
GRADE: C

No.: GB-154
NAME: Burma-Shave Half Pound
HEIGHT: 3⅝"
SLOT: non-slotted
INFO: Lid — rumored that it is found
slotted; also Burma-Shave One
Pound, 4⅛", rumored that it is found
slotted
GRADE: B

No.: GB-155
NAME: Atlas Round Strong
Shoulder Mason
HEIGHT: 3⅝"
SLOT: punched
INFO: Lid — Zinc; P. of H.
Washington, Pa., 1938
GRADE: D

No.: GB-156
NAME: Atlas Mason
HEIGHT: 3¾"
SLOT: punched
INFO: square; Lid —
Zinc; 65th Annual Conven-
tion A.F.G.W.U., June 30
– July 1, 1941, Washing-
ton, Penna.
GRADE: D

No.: GB-157
NAME: Atlas Mason
HEIGHT: 3¾"
SLOT: punched
INFO: square; Lid — two
piece brass; Lid — Atlas
Seal-All, Arc
GRADE: B

See page 7 for price ranges.

No.: GB-158
NAME: Atlas Strong Shoulder
        Mason
HEIGHT: 3⅝"
SLOT: punched
INFO: round; Lid — zinc
GRADE: B

No.: GB-159
NAME: Atlas Strong Shoulder
        Mason
HEIGHT: 3⅝"
SLOT: punched
INFO: round; Lid — zinc;
G.A.R. Encampment, Washington, Pa., 1938
GRADE: D

No.: GB-160
NAME: Atlas Strong Shoulder
        Mason
HEIGHT: 3⅝"
SLOT: punched
INFO: round; Lid — two piece
brass; Protected Home, Circle
No. 91, Oct. 2, 1939
GRADE: D

No.: GB-161
NAME: Burn Ohio Coal Mason
HEIGHT: 3⅝"
SLOT: punched
INFO: round; Lid — zinc
GRADE: D

No.: GB-162
NAME: Zanesville 1942 Mason
HEIGHT: 3⅝"
SLOT: punched
INFO: round; Lid — zinc; Start
Saving Now For Zanesville in
1942, Chamber of Commerce
GRADE: D

No.: GB-163
NAME: Atlas Mason
HEIGHT: 3¾"
SLOT: punched
INFO: square variation; Lid —
two piece brass; Atlas Mason,
Seal-All
GRADE: B

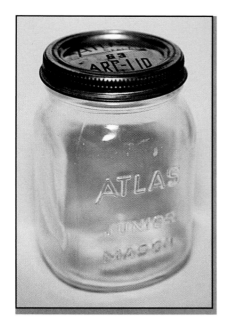

NO.: GB-164
NAME: Atlas Junior Mason
HEIGHT: 4½"
SLOT: converted
INFO: Lid — two-piece brass plated; Atlas Seal-All, 63, Arc-Lid
GRADE: C

NO.: GB-165
NAME: Liberty Bell
HEIGHT: 2⅜"
SLOT: converted
INFO: Lid — brass plated; Pass and Stow, Philada., MDCCLIII, 1776
GRADE: C

NO.: GB-166
NAME: Square Shoulder
HEIGHT: 4⅝"
SLOT: punched
INFO: Lid — white; Bottom — Consumers Glass Co. Ltd., 1978
GRADE: C

NO.: GB-167
NAME: Hip Sided
HEIGHT: 3⅜"
SLOT: punched
INFO: Lid — black tin; initials glued on glass, T.R.C.
GRADE: C

NO.: GB-168
NAME: Instant Money Coffee
HEIGHT: 4½"
SLOT: punched
INFO: Lid — white; Suffolk Franklin Savings Bank
GRADE: D

See page 7 for price ranges.

NO.: GB-169
NAME: Coin-shaped decanter
HEIGHT: 4⅞"
SLOT: questionable
INFO: Lid — black tin
GRADE: C

No.: GB-170
NAME: Victory Thrift Jar
HEIGHT: 6¼"
SLOT: punched
INFO: Lid — white tin; molded pictures of planes, tanks, ships; Label — paper
GRADE: Rare

No.: GB-171
NAME: A Drop in the Jar
HEIGHT: 6⅞"
SLOT: punched
INFO: Lid — tin; Label — paper; 1 Penny a Meal, Every Time You Eat a Meal Give a Penny For the Unemployed
GRADE: D

No.: GB-172
NAME: A Penny A Meal
HEIGHT: 3⅛"
SLOT: punched
INFO: Lid — embossed aluminum; Label — paper; A Penny A Meal, Olivet Mortgage Interest Fund, Freely Ye Have Received, Freely Give
GRADE: C

No.: GB-173
NAME: Isabelle Orphanage
HEIGHT: 3"
SLOT: punched
INFO: Lid — black tin; Label — One Penny a Day You Can Be the Supporter of the Isabelle Orphanage, Pusan, Korea; Korea Gospel Mission Inc., P.O. Box 291, Inglewood, CA
GRADE: C

No.: GB-174
NAME: Building Fund
HEIGHT: 3¼"
SLOT: punched
INFO: Lid — gold tin; Label — paper; and let the house of God be builded
GRADE: C

No.: GB-175
NAME: Mickey Mouse jelly jar
HEIGHT: 6"
SLOT: punched
INFO: Lid — red, black, gold or red, black, silver, embossed Mickey, Feed Mickey for Wealth, Eat Jam for Health; molded pictures of Mickey, Minnie, Pluto, and Horace
GRADE: E

No.: GB-176
NAME: Standard Parts
HEIGHT: 4¼"
SLOT: punched
INFO: Lid — black, gold, Standard Motor Products; Label — Standard Motor Prod. Inc., Long Island City, N.Y., Seattle, Wash.
GRADE: C

No.: GB-177
NAME: Barbasol
HEIGHT: 3⅜"
SLOT: punched and non-slotted
INFO: large; Lid — black, white
GRADE: C

No.: GB-178
NAME: Barbasol
HEIGHT: 3"
SLOT: punched and non-slotted
INFO: medium; Lid — black, white
GRADE: C

No.: GB-179
NAME: Barbasol
HEIGHT: 2"
SLOT: not yet found punched
INFO: small; Lid — black, white
GRADE: C

No.: GB-180
NAME: Molle'
HEIGHT: 2"
SLOT: punched, questionable
INFO: small; Lid — brown, cream
GRADE: C

No.: GB-181
NAME: Mollé
HEIGHT: 2¾"
SLOT: non-slotted
INFO: medium, Lid — brown, cream; not yet found punched
GRADE: B

No.: GB-182
NAME: Mollé
HEIGHT: 3¼"
SLOT: non-slotted
INFO: large; Lid — brown, cream; not yet found punched
GRADE: B

RATING, GRADING	
A	To $15.00
B	$15.00 – 35.00
C	$35.00 – 75.00
D	$75.00 – 150.00
E	$150.00 – 300.00
F	$300.00 – 600.00
Rare	$600.00 – 1,000.00
Very Rare	negotiable

No.: GB-183
NAME: Eagle jelly jar
HEIGHT: 3⅜"
SLOT: punched
INFO: vertical ribbed glass; Lid — embossed tin, probably punched after market
GRADE: D

No.: GB-184
NAME: Eagle jelly jar
HEIGHT: 3"
SLOT: punched
INFO: square pattern glass; Lid — embossed tin, probably punched after market
GRADE: D

No.: GB-185
NAME: Jelly mug
HEIGHT: 3⅛"
SLOT: punched
INFO: Lid — plain tin; pressed glass
GRADE: D

NO.: GB-186
NAME: Eagle jelly jar
HEIGHT: 3⅜"
SLOT: punched
INFO: plain glass; Lid — embossed tin, probably punched after market
GRADE: D

NO.: GB-187
NAME: Dr. Ellis' Curlast Wave Set
HEIGHT: 5¾"
SLOT: punched for comb
INFO: Lid — gold, white
GRADE: D

NO.: GB-188
NAME: Dr. Ellis' Wave Set
HEIGHT: 6⅛"
SLOT: punched rough
INFO: Lid — gold; molded glass with picture of bottle and comb on back
GRADE: C

NO.: GB-189
NAME: Pink Girl Shmoo
HEIGHT: 7⅛"
SLOT: punched and non-slotted
INFO: Lids — pink slotted, blue non-slotted; Bottom — Baldwin Laboratories, Saegertown, PA.
GRADE: F

NO.: GB-190
NAME: Blue Boy Shmoo
HEIGHT: 7⅛"
SLOT: punched and non-slotted
INFO: Lids — light blue slotted, red non-slotted; Bottom — Baldwin Laboratories, Saegertown, PA.
GRADE: F

NO.: GB-191
NAME: Flapper Girl
HEIGHT: 10¾"
SLOT: punched and non-slotted
INFO: Lids — flat punched, domed non-slotted, paper face inside glass; Label — paper belt, MFD. by Bradle & Smith Co., Philadelphia, PA., Net Wt. 1 lb., Des Pat. 84161
GRADE: D

NO.: GB-192
NAME: Moose Lodge 1937
HEIGHT: 3⅞"
SLOT: punched
INFO: Lid — tin; N.J. State Convention, Bridgeton, N.J. 1937, L.O.O.M, No. 322
GRADE: D

NO.: GB-193
NAME: Popeye & Olive
HEIGHT: 5½"
SLOT: molded in lid
INFO: Lid — black plastic combination locking; screened figures on glass; originally held Chocoballs, Oriental label
GRADE: F

NO.: GB-194
NAME: Alton Onized Santa
HEIGHT: 6¼"
SLOT: punched
INFO: Lid — red tin; Front — XMAS Greetings, Alton Onized Club; Back — Save Your Pennies
GRADE: E

NO.: GB-195
NAME: Old Woman in the Shoe
HEIGHT: 7⅛"
SLOT: punched
INFO: Lid — red tin; pyroglazed white, blue, poem, kids with the bank in their hands
GRADE: E

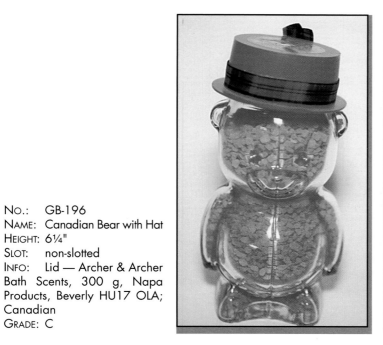

RATING, GRADING	
A	To $15.00
B	$15.00 – 35.00
C	$35.00 – 75.00
D	$75.00 – 150.00
E	$150.00 – 300.00
F	$300.00 – 600.00
Rare	$600.00 – 1,000.00
Very Rare	negotiable

No.: GB-196
NAME: Canadian Bear with Hat
HEIGHT: 6¼"
SLOT: non-slotted
INFO: Lid — Archer & Archer Bath Scents, 300 g, Napa Products, Beverly HU17 OLA; Canadian
GRADE: C

No.: GB-197
NAME: Sweet Queen
HEIGHT: 5"
SLOT: punched
INFO: Lid — white tin; Label — paper, several variations; Packed by Kitchen Star Food Prod, Cliffside Park, New Jersey
GRADE: C

No.: GB-198
NAME: Smiling Jack
HEIGHT: 8½"
SLOT: punched and non-slotted
INFO: Lid — plain tin, found machine and hand punched; frosted glass with the head hand painted
GRADE: F

No.: GB-199
NAME: Smiling Jack
HEIGHT: 8½"
SLOT: punched and non-slotted
INFO: clear glass; Lid — plain tin, hand punched
GRADE: E

No.: GB-200
NAME: Likker Kitty, large
HEIGHT: 9⅜"
SLOT: punched
INFO: cocktail shaker; Lid — brass, slotted with pouring spout; frosted on outside of glass with screened coins, cat, and Emergency Use, Remove Coins Place Thumb Over Slot and Shake Vigorously
GRADE: E

No.: GB-201
NAME: Likker Kitty, small
HEIGHT: 7⅝"
SLOT: punched
INFO: cocktail shaker; Lid — brass, slotted with pouring spout; frosted inside white with screened coins, cat, and Emergency Use, black and gold colors for cat
GRADE: E

No.: GB-202
NAME: Stow Aways Little Pig
HEIGHT: 5³⁄₁₆"
SLOT: punched
INFO: Lid — tin, Brother Can You Spare a Coin; Back Label — Allen's Wholesale, Jelly Beans ½ lb Net.; paper glasses on front of face; A.W. Allen Ltd. Melbourne
GRADE: F

No.: GB-203
NAME: Stow Aways Little Pig
HEIGHT: 5³⁄₁₆"
SLOT: punched
INFO: Lid — tin, Brother Can You Spare a Coin; Allen's For Sweets in glass on bottom, same as GB-202; A.W. Allen Ltd. Melbourne
GRADE: F

No.: GB-204
NAME: Ma Brown Apple Butter
HEIGHT: 4½"
SLOT: converted
INFO: Lid — litho, Ma Brown Apple Butter, Squire Dingee Co, Chicago, Ill, punched after market; apple shaped
GRADE: C

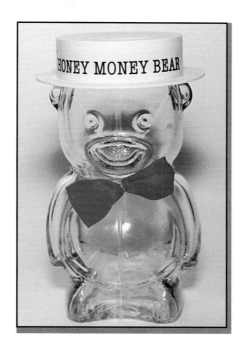

NO.: GB-205
NAME: Ship decanter
HEIGHT: 9⅜"
SLOT: cut in glass
INFO: Lid — glass drinking cup inverted; blue glass with screened images of ship
GRADE: C

NO.: GB-206
NAME: Honey Money Bear
HEIGHT: 5⅝"
SLOT: molded in plastic hat
INFO: Lid — plastic straw hat with clear plastic label printed in black; ribbon bow tie with gold elastic neck band
GRADE: D

NO.: GB-207
NAME: Taiwan Lion
HEIGHT: 7³⁄₁₆"
SLOT: punched
INFO: Lid — white tin; Bottom — Made in Taiwan, Vandor 1974
GRADE: D

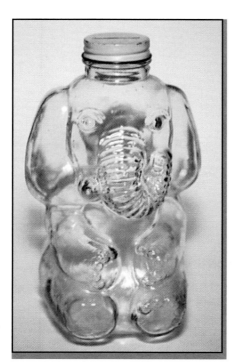

NO.: GB-208
NAME: Taiwan Elephant
HEIGHT: 7"
SLOT: punched
INFO: Lid — white tin; Bottom — Made in Taiwan, Vandor 1974
GRADE: E

NO.: GB-209
NAME: Taiwan Bear
HEIGHT: 7"
SLOT: punched
INFO: Lid — white tin; Bottom — Made in Taiwan, TPNF
GRADE: F

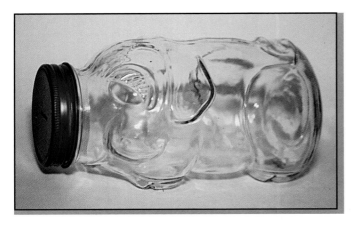

NO.: GB-210
NAME: Libbey of Canada Pig
HEIGHT: 7½"
SLOT: punched and non-slotted
INFO: Lid — green tin, found slotted with tin lid, found non-slotted with plastic lid; height measured standing on end; Libbey of Canada under nose
GRADE: C

NO.: GB-211
NAME: 1929 Car
HEIGHT: 4¾"
SLOT: punched and non-slotted
INFO: Lid — white tin with liner, found with black plastic, non-slotted lid; height measured standing on end; below grill marked FP 1929
GRADE: B

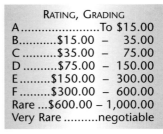

RATING, GRADING	
A	To $15.00
B	$15.00 – 35.00
C	$35.00 – 75.00
D	$75.00 – 150.00
E	$150.00 – 300.00
F	$300.00 – 600.00
Rare	$600.00 – 1,000.00
Very Rare	negotiable

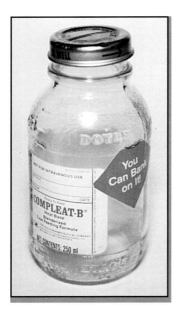

NO.: GB-212
NAME: Doyle Compleat-B
HEIGHT: 5"
SLOT: punched
INFO: Lid — tin; Label — Doyle Compleat-B, Meat Base, You Can Bank On It
GRADE: C

NO.: GB-213
NAME: Ten Bears jar
HEIGHT: 5¾"
SLOT: punched
INFO: Lid — black tin; questionable; Bottom — Des Pat No. 100306
GRADE: C

NO.: GB-214
NAME: Bank on Jelly Beans
HEIGHT: 4½"
SLOT: punched
INFO: Lid — yellow plastic; etched in glass
GRADE: C

No.: GB-215
Name: Mickey's Malt Liquor
Height: 5⅜"
Slot: punched
Info: Lid — white plastic; green glass
Grade: C

No.: GB-216
Name: Modern jelly jar
Height: 4⅞"
Slot: punched
Info: Lid — white plastic; pressed glass
Grade: C

No.: GB-217
Name: George Washington 1732 – 1932
Height: 7⅞"
Slot: converted?
Info: Lid — black tin, found with black plastic, non-slotted lid
Grade: C

No.: GB-218
Name: Steubenville Milk Fund
Height: 5½"
Slot: punched
Info: Lid — red tin not original, has not been found with original lid; Back — boy in swing, Help Them to Happiness with a Strong Body
Grade: C

No.: GB-219
Name: "Mule Kick" Creme Polish
Height: 3⅝"
Slot: converted
Info: Lid — black, white tin, "Mule Kick" Creme Polish, A Beauty Treatment for Bath Tubs, Sinks, Floors, Etc.; J.A. Sexauer Mfg Co Inc., New York, 14 oz
Grade: C

NO.: GB-220
NAME: Amber Horseshoe
HEIGHT: 5"
SLOT: punched and non-slotted
INFO: large; Lid — plain tin, converted?
GRADE: C

NO.: GB-221
NAME: Amber Horseshoe
HEIGHT: 4"
SLOT: punched and non-slotted
INFO: small; Lid — plain tin, converted?
GRADE: C

NO.: GB-222
NAME: Your Future
HEIGHT: 6¼"
SLOT: punched
INFO: Lid — white tin; Your Future Depends on Buying Habits as Well as Saving Habits
GRADE: C

RATING, GRADING	
A	To $15.00
B	$15.00 – 35.00
C	$35.00 – 75.00
D	$75.00 – 150.00
E	$150.00 – 300.00
F	$300.00 – 600.00
Rare	$600.00 – 1,000.00
Very Rare	negotiable

NO.: GB-223
NAME: Lions Club White Cane
HEIGHT: 5⁵⁄₁₆"
SLOT: punched
INFO: Lid — red, white tin
GRADE: D

NO.: GB-224
NAME: Bingo Bucks
HEIGHT: 6¼"
SLOT: non-slotted
INFO: Lid — white plastic with figures attached on metal lid
GRADE: B

NO.: GB-225
NAME: Girl Face jar
HEIGHT: 4⅛"
SLOT: punched
INFO: Lid — white tin; eyes and mouth heavy paper glued on
GRADE: C

NO.: GB-226
NAME: Florida jar
HEIGHT: 4"
SLOT: punched and non-slotted
INFO: Lid — tin lithographed found punched and non-slotted; same jar also found for other states
GRADE: C

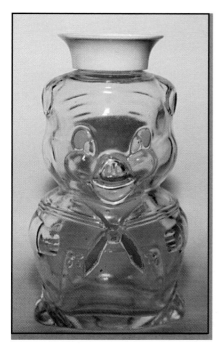

NO.: GB-227
NAME: Pig in Sailor Suit
HEIGHT: 5"
SLOT: punched or molded?
INFO: Lid — white plastic sailor hat; yellow and white painted eyes, mouth, and scarf; England
GRADE: D

NO.: GB-228
NAME: Pin Money Jar
HEIGHT: 4¾"
SLOT: non-slotted
INFO: Lid — tin litho non-slotted; Pin Money Pickles, Founded 1868
GRADE: D

NO.: GB-229
NAME: Bunco Bucks!
HEIGHT: 6¼"
SLOT: non-sotted
INFO: Lid — white plastic with figures attached on metal lid
GRADE: B

NO.: GB-230
NAME: Glass Bucket
HEIGHT: 6½"
SLOT: punched
INFO: Lid — tin painted green slot is questionable
GRADE: B

NO.: GB-231
NAME: La Suprema Clock
HEIGHT: 4⅜"
SLOT: non-slotted
INFO: Lid — litho tin picture of woman and two children; plastic neck carry band with strap, says "SUPREMA"; Fabrica De Ce Jetas, Carmen C. Vda. De. Macias
GRADE: D

NO.: GB-232
NAME: Stewart's Root Beer
HEIGHT: 5⅛"
SLOT: punched
INFO: Lid — white tin; dark amber glass
GRADE: B

NO.: GB-233
NAME: Popeye Golf Bag
HEIGHT: 5½"
SLOT: molded in lid
INFO: Lid — white plastic combination locking; screened figures on glass; came with plastic medallion
GRADE: F

Kraft Food and CPC International

No.: KIGB-1
Name: Kraft Snowman
Height: 6"
Slot: non-slotted
Info: Lid — red, white litho; Kraft twist-on lid; converted slot
Grade: B

No.: KIGB-2
Name: Kraft Santa Claus
Height: 6⅛"
Slot: non-slotted
Info: Lid — red, white litho, Kraft twist-on lid, grape jelly Santa jar, 32 oz
Grade: B

No.: KIGB-3
Name: Mario Cheez Whiz
Height: 6¾"
Slot: non-slotted
Info: Lid — yellow, red, black tin, Kraft Canadian, French and English; Cheez Whiz Process Cheese Spread; Bottom — Kraft 1989
Grade: D

Photo Not Available
No.: KIGB-4
Name: Kraft Mrs. Santa
Height: 6⅛"
Slot: non-slotted
Info: Lid — red, white litho, Kraft twist-on lid
Grade: D

No.: KIGB-5
Name: Kraft Dinosaur
Height: 5⅜"
Slot: non-slotted
Info: Lid — magenta, white tin, Kraft twist-on; converted
Grade: B

Rating, Grading	
A	To $15.00
B	$15.00 – 35.00
C	$35.00 – 75.00
D	$75.00 – 150.00
E	$150.00 – 300.00
F	$300.00 – 600.00
Rare	$600.00 – 1,000.00
Very Rare	negotiable

NO.: KIGB-6
NAME: Kraft Four Button Bear
HEIGHT: 6"
SLOT: non-slotted
INFO: Lid — purple, red, white, Kraft twist-on; Bottom — 3" circle plain or 2½" circle Kraft 1988
GRADE: B

NO.: KIGB-7
NAME: Yogi Bear Head
HEIGHT: 5⅝"
SLOT: marked for punch out slot
INFO: Lid — red or green plastic; Bottom — Kraft 1989; peanut butter
GRADE: D

NO.: KIGB-8
NAME: Bear with Pacifier
HEIGHT: 5⅜"
SLOT: non-slotted
INFO: Lid — black, white, gold tin twist, Kraft Canadian, French and English; Bottom — Kraft 1988; jelly
GRADE: C

NO.: KIGB-9
NAME: Skippy Chipmunk
HEIGHT: 6½"
SLOT: slot under label
INFO: Lid — blue plastic; 1990 CPC International Special Edition, 100th Birthday of Peanut Butter
GRADE: A

NO.: KIGB-10
NAME: Kraft Bow Tie Bear
HEIGHT: 7¼"
SLOT: punched
INFO: Lid — green plastic, Lukian Plastic Toronto, Montreal – Made in Canada; peanut butter
GRADE: C

NO.: KIGB-11
NAME: Kraft Necklace Girl Bear
HEIGHT: 7¼"
SLOT: punched
INFO: Lid — green plastic, Lukian Plastic Toronto, Montreal – Made in Canada; peanut butter
GRADE: C

NO.: KIGB-12
NAME: Kraft Grandma Knitting
HEIGHT: 6⅛"
SLOT: slot under label
INFO: Lid — green plastic, Kraft Canadian, French and English; peanut butter
GRADE: C

NO.: KIGB-13
NAME: Kraft Bear with Peanut
HEIGHT: 7¼"
SLOT: slot under label
INFO: Lid — red plastic, Kraft Canadian, French and English; crunchy peanut butter
GRADE: D

NO.: KIGB-14
NAME: Skippy Bear with Pot
HEIGHT: 7¼"
SLOT: non-slotted
INFO: Lid — dark blue, white plastic, Super Chunk Peanut Butter, 48 oz
GRADE: A

NO.: KIGB-15
NAME: Kraft Bear with Peanut
HEIGHT: 7¼"
SLOT: slot under label
INFO: Label — green plastic, Kraft Canadian, French and English; smooth peanut butter
GRADE: D

Baby Bottle Banks

A Guide to American Nursing Bottles

Variation: SAMUEL CALLET CO. PGH., PA., embossed vertically on the bank. The base is embossed with tiny dots.
Note: These bottles frequently were made with advertising alone or in conjunction with the nursery character pictured.
They were pyroglazed in a great variety of colors. A list of the known designs follows:

1. A Boy Can Dream If He Wants To
2. A Girl Can Dream If She Wants To
3. Athlete (young boy in baseball uniform)
4. Baa-Baa Black Sheep
5. Baby Bear
6. Baby's Face
7. Beauty and the Beast
8. Cinderella
9. Circus Train
10. Clown (not Da-Da)
11. Cowboy
12. Cowgirl
13. Da-Da (clown)
14. Dancer (young girl)
15. The Elves (working on a shoe)
16. Elf (standing facing front)
17. Engineer
18. Feeling of Security
19. Golden Goose
20. Goldilocks
21. Goosey Gander
22. Hansel and Gretel
23. Humpty Dumpty
24. Jack and the Beanstalk
25. Jack and Jill
26. Jack Be Nimble
27. Knox Glass Inc. (picture of bowling elf)
28. Little Boy Blue
29. Little Jack Horner
30. Little Miss Muffet
31. The Little Red Hen
32. Little Red Riding Hood
33. Little Sweetheart Drink
34. Majorette
35. Make Mine Milk
36. Mama Bear
37. Mary Had a Little Lamb
38. Mother It's Feeding Time Again
39. Nurse
40. Old King Cole
41. Old Mother Hubbard
42. Papa Bear
43. Party Boy
44. Party Girl
45. Peter Rabbit
46. Plane
47. The Prince
48. Puss in Boots
49. Robbie Yum Yum
50. Saving for the Future
51. Sing a Song of Six Pence
52. Sleeping Beauty
53. Soldier (young boy in soldier's uniform)
54. Teacher
55. Time for Re-fill
56. This Little Pig Had Roast Beef
57. This Little Pig Stayed Home
58. This Little Pig Went to Market
59. Three Little Pigs (building brickhouse)
60. To Her Highness
61. To His Majesty
62. Tom Thumb
63. Your Angel Child

(106) Samuel Callet Co.
Pittsburg, Pennsylvania
Embossed on the base
Screw neck wide mouth
Circa 1950 to 1970
Clear, rounded rectangle
8 ounce scale
5 raised ridges on the curved sides
Pyroglazed with pictures of nursery characters
Fittings: Searer Rubber Co. plastic screw ring,
disc, and a pop-up nipple

NO.: BBGB-1
NAME: Smith's Milk
HEIGHT: 6½"
SLOT: punched
INFO: Lid — blue tin; Bottom — Samuel Callet Co, PGH, PA
GRADE: C

NO.: BBGB-2
NAME: Millers Furniture Brownie
HEIGHT: 6½"
SLOT: punched
INFO: Lid — white tin; Samuel Callet Co, PGH, PA
GRADE: C

NO.: BBGB-3
NAME: To Her Highness
HEIGHT: 6½"
SLOT: punched
INFO: Lid — white tin with celluloid collar; Samuel Callet Co, PGH, PA
GRADE: C

NO.: BBGB-4
NAME: Brokhoff's Dairy, Jack Be Nimble
HEIGHT: 6½"
SLOT: punched
INFO: Lid — blue tin; Samuel Callet Co, PGH, PA
GRADE: C

NO.: BBGB-5
NAME: To His Majesty
HEIGHT: 6½"
SLOT: punched
INFO: Lid — blue tin; Samuel Callet Co, PGH, PA
GRADE: C

NO.: BBGB-6
NAME: Goosey Gander
HEIGHT: 6½"
SLOT: punched
INFO: Lid — blue tin, not usually found with bank lid; Samuel Callet Co, PGH, PA
GRADE: C

NO.: BBGB-7
NAME: Jack and the Beanstalk
HEIGHT: 6½"
SLOT: punched
INFO: Lid — blue tin; not usually found with bank lid; Samuel Callet Co, PGH, PA
GRADE: C

NO.: BBGB-8
NAME: Bupp's Milk, Humpty Dumpty
HEIGHT: 6½"
SLOT: punched
INFO: Lid — blue tin; Samuel Callet Co, PGH, PA
GRADE: C

NO.: BBGB-9
NAME: B.A. Meyer Co. Jewelers
HEIGHT: 6½"
SLOT: punched
INFO: Lid — white tin; Samuel Callet Co, PGH, PA
GRADE: C

RATING, GRADING	
A	To $15.00
B	$15.00 – 35.00
C	$35.00 – 75.00
D	$75.00 – 150.00
E	$150.00 – 300.00
F	$300.00 – 600.00
Rare	$600.00 – 1,000.00
Very Rare	negotiable

NO.: BBGB-10
NAME: Martz's Milk Baby Face
HEIGHT: 6½"
SLOT: punched
INFO: Lid — blue tin; Samuel Callet Co, PGH, PA
GRADE: C

NO.: BBGB-11
NAME: Loving Furniture Clown
HEIGHT: 6½"
SLOT: punched
INFO: Lid — blue tin; Samuel Callet Co, PGH, PA
GRADE: C

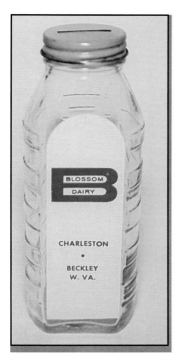

No.: BBGB-12
NAME: Blossom Dairy
HEIGHT: 6½"
SLOT: punched
INFO: Lid — blue tin; Samuel Callet Co, PGH, PA
GRADE: C

No.: BBGB-13
NAME: Brokhoff's Dairy Goldilocks
HEIGHT: 6½"
SLOT: punched
INFO: Lid — blue tin; Samuel Callet Co, PGH, PA
GRADE: C

No.: BBGB-14
NAME: Brokhoff's Dairy Little Miss Muffet
HEIGHT: 6½"
SLOT: punched
INFO: Lid — blue tin; Samuel Callet Co, PGH, PA
GRADE: C

No.: BBGB-15
NAME: Loving Furniture Clown
HEIGHT: 6½"
SLOT: punched
INFO: Lid — blue tin; Samuel Callet Co, PGH, PA
GRADE: C

No.: BBGB-16
NAME: Green's Dairy Rooster
HEIGHT: 6½"
SLOT: punched
INFO: Lid — blue tin with celluloid collar; Samuel Callet Co, PGH, PA
GRADE: C

NO.: BBGB-17
NAME: Dietrich's Milk, To His Majesty
HEIGHT: 6½"
SLOT: punched
INFO: Lid — blue tin; Samuel Callet Co, PGH, PA
GRADE: C

NO.: BBGB-18
NAME: Shamokin Milk Baby Face
HEIGHT: 6½"
SLOT: punched
INFO: Lid — white tin; Samuel Callet Co, PGH, PA
GRADE: C

NO.: BBGB-19
NAME: "A Boy Can Dream If He Wants To"
HEIGHT: 6½"
SLOT: punched
INFO: Lid — blue tin; Samuel Callet Co, PGH, PA
GRADE: C

NO.: BBGB-20
NAME: Cream Top Dairy
HEIGHT: 4¾"
SLOT: punched
INFO: Lid — blue tin with celluloid collar
GRADE: D

RATING, GRADING	
A	To $15.00
B	$15.00 – 35.00
C	$35.00 – 75.00
D	$75.00 – 150.00
E	$150.00 – 300.00
F	$300.00 – 600.00
Rare	$600.00 – 1,000.00
Very Rare	negotiable

NO.: BBGB-21
NAME: Eby's Dairy Baby Face
HEIGHT: 6⅜"
SLOT: punched
INFO: Lid — blue tin
GRADE: D

NO.: BBGB-22
NAME: Martz's Dairy Goldilocks
HEIGHT: 6½"
SLOT: punched
INFO: Lid — blue tin; Samuel Callet Co, PGH, PA
GRADE: C

NO.: BBGB-23
NAME: Robbie Yum Yum
HEIGHT: 6½"
SLOT: punched
INFO: Lid — blue tin; Samuel
Callet Co, PGH, PA
GRADE: C

NO.: BBGB-24
NAME: Oneida Dairy Baby Face
HEIGHT: 6½"
SLOT: punched
INFO: Lid — blue tin; Samuel
Callet Co, PGH, PA
GRADE: C

NO.: BBGB-25
NAME: Rothermel's Dairy, To
His Majesty
HEIGHT: 6½"
SLOT: punched
INFO: Lid — blue tin; Samuel
Callet Co, PGH, PA
GRADE: C

NO.: BBGB-26
NAME: Da-Da Clown
HEIGHT: 6½"
SLOT: punched
INFO: Lid — white tin;
Samuel Callet Co, PGH, PA
GRADE: C

NO.: BBGB-27
NAME: The Elves Repairing
Shoe
HEIGHT: 6½"
SLOT: punched
INFO: Lid — blue tin;
Samuel Callet Co, PGH, PA
GRADE: C

Milk Bottle Banks

NO.: MBGB-1
NAME: We Must Stop Inflation
HEIGHT: 4½"
SLOT: punched
INFO: half pint; Lid — one-piece steel with lock; decal label, painted white inside; Back — Submarine Base Credit Union, Groton, Conn.
GRADE: C

NO.: MBGB-2
NAME: Save For a Rainy Day Cow
HEIGHT: 4½"
SLOT: punched
INFO: half pint; Lid — one-piece steel with lock; decal label; Bower Mfg. Co., Goshen, Ind.
GRADE: B

NO.: MBGB-3
NAME: Boy Waving Shirt Out
HEIGHT: 4½"
SLOT: punched
INFO: half pint; Lid — one-piece steel with lock; decal label; Bower Mfg. Co, Goshen, Ind.
GRADE: C

NO.: MBGB-4
NAME: Boy with Straw Hat
HEIGHT: 4½"
SLOT: punched
INFO: half pint; Lid — red plastic, For a Rainy Day Save $50.00; Bower Mfg. Co, Goshen, Ind.; Pat No. 2,709,037
GRADE: C

NO.: MBGB-5
NAME: Boy Holding Large Coin
HEIGHT: 4½"
SLOT: punched
INFO: half pint; Lid — two-piece steel with lock; metallic label front and back; Bower Mfg. Co, Goshen, Ind.
GRADE: B

NO.: MBGB-6
NAME: Eagle Facing Right
HEIGHT: 4½"
SLOT: punched
INFO: half pint; Lid — one-piece steel with lock; decal label; Back — Provident National Bank, CALN Office, Thorndale, Penn., 19372
GRADE: B

NO.: MBGB-7
NAME: Boy Holding Large Coin
HEIGHT: 4½"
SLOT: punched
INFO: Lid — one-piece steel with lock; metallic label front and back; Back label — amount of money bank will hold by coin denomination
GRADE: A

NO.: MBGB-8
NAME: Pioneer Milk Fund
HEIGHT: 4½"
SLOT: punched
INFO: half pint; Lid — one-piece steel with lock; decal label; Back label — milk benefits for children
GRADE: C

See page 7 for price ranges.

NO.: MBGB-9
NAME: Whitestone Farms
HEIGHT: 4½"
SLOT: punched
INFO: half pint; Lid — one-piece steel with lock; screened label; Back — Your Bottle Bank, Daily savings in this bottle bank will help pay for the milk you drank
GRADE: D

NO.: MBGB-10
NAME: Uncle Sam Banner
HEIGHT: 4½"
SLOT: punched
INFO: half pint; Lid — one-piece steel with lock; decal label
GRADE: D

No.: MBGB-11
NAME: Uncle Sam 1776 – 1976
HEIGHT: 4½"
SLOT: punched
INFO: half pint; Lid — one-piece
steel with lock; decal label; painted
white inside
GRADE: D

No.: MBGB-12
NAME: Bowman Dairy Company
HEIGHT: 4¾"
SLOT: punched
INFO: half pint; Lid — two-piece steel
with lock
GRADE: C

No.: MBGB-13
NAME: Franklin Lake Milk
HEIGHT: 4¼"
SLOT: punched
INFO: half pint; Lid — metallic
foil
GRADE: C

No.: MBGB-14
NAME: Sun Crest Keep em Flying
HEIGHT: 5½"
SLOT: punched
INFO: tall half pint; Lid — two-piece
steel with lock
GRADE: D

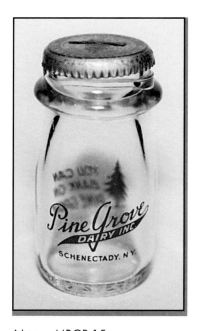

No.: MBGB-15
NAME: Pine Grove Dairy
HEIGHT: 4¼"
SLOT: punched
INFO: half pint; Lid — metallic
foil
GRADE: C

NO.:   MBGB-16
NAME: Community Ambulance Fund
HEIGHT: 4½"
SLOT: punched
INFO: half pint; Lid — one-piece steel with lock; decal label
GRADE: D

NO.:   MBGB-17
NAME: Voegel's Milk
HEIGHT: 5½"
SLOT: punched
INFO: tall half pint; Lid — one-piece steel with lock; painted white inside
GRADE: C

NO.:   MBGB-18
NAME: Geographical Center of North America
HEIGHT: 5½"
SLOT: punched
INFO: tall half pint; Lid — one-piece steel with lock; decal label; painted white inside
GRADE: D

NO.:   MBGB-19
NAME: Change for the Baby
HEIGHT: 8¾"
SLOT: punched
INFO: quart; Lid — one-piece steel with lock; decal label; painted white inside; Bower Mfg. Co., Goshen, Ind.
GRADE: C

NO.:   MBGB-20
NAME: Save For a Rainy Day Cow
HEIGHT: 8¾"
SLOT: punched
INFO: quart; Lid — one-piece steel with lock; decal label; painted white inside; Bower Mfg. Co., Goshen, Ind.
GRADE: C

NO.: MBGB-21
NAME: Social Security Man, Boat
HEIGHT: 8¾"
SLOT: punched
INFO: quart; Lid — one-piece steel with lock; decal label; painted white inside; Bower Mfg. Co., Goshen, Ind.
GRADE: C

NO.: MBGB-22
NAME: Saving For New Wheels
HEIGHT: 8¾"
SLOT: punched
INFO: quart; Lid — one-piece steel with lock; decal label; painted white inside; Bower Mfg. Co., Goshen, Ind.
GRADE: C

NO.: MBGB-23
NAME: Moola Cow
HEIGHT: 8¾"
SLOT: punched
INFO: quart; Lid — one-piece steel with lock; decal label; painted white inside; Bower Mfg. Co., Goshen, Ind.
GRADE: C

NO.: MBGB-24
NAME: Fat Cat
HEIGHT: 8¾"
SLOT: punched
INFO: quart; Lid — one-piece steel with lock; decal label; painted white inside; Bower Mfg. Co., Goshen, Ind.
GRADE: C

NO.: MBGB-25
NAME: Reiter Dairy
HEIGHT: 4½"
SLOT: punched
INFO: half pint; Lid — one-piece steel with lock; paper label; painted white inside
GRADE: D

NO.:   MBGB-26
NAME: Parker City Pennsylva-
       nia Centennial Bank
HEIGHT: 8¾"
SLOT: punched
INFO: quart; Lid — one-
piece steel with lock; Glass
Containers Corp., Parker, Pa.
GRADE: E

NO.:   MBGB-27
NAME: Buy War Bonds &
       Stamps
HEIGHT: 9½"
SLOT: punched
INFO: quart; Lid — one-
piece steel with lock; Mid-
west Pasteurized Milk;
Midwest Dairy Products Co.
GRADE: D

NO.:   MBGB-28
NAME: Foghorn Leghorn
       Moo!
HEIGHT: 8¹¹⁄₁₆"
SLOT: non-slotted
INFO: quart; Lid — red plas-
tic; Acme Dairy Farms, Inc.;
Tm Warner Bros. 1996
GRADE: C

NO.:   MBGB-29
NAME: Niagra Falls
       Canada
HEIGHT: 8¾"
SLOT: punched
INFO: quart; Lid — one-
piece steel with lock;
paper label; painted white
inside
GRADE: C

RATING, GRADING	
A	To $15.00
B	$15.00 – 35.00
C	$35.00 – 75.00
D	$75.00 – 150.00
E	$150.00 – 300.00
F	$300.00 – 600.00
Rare	$600.00 – 1,000.00
Very Rare	negotiable

NO.: MBGB-30
NAME: Milk For Needy Children
HEIGHT: 7⁹⁄₁₆"
SLOT: punched
INFO: pint; Lid — two-piece steel with hold down straps and lock, wooden base; paper label, Seattle Milk Fund; Main 3-7632
GRADE: D

NO.: MBGB-31
NAME: Sweet Cream Cow
HEIGHT: 10⅛"
SLOT: punched
INFO: half gallon; Lid — one-piece steel with lock, red plastic handle; decal label; painted white inside; Bower Mfg. Co., Goshen, Ind.
GRADE: C

NO.: MBGB-32
NAME: Stork Stuff
HEIGHT: 10⅛"
SLOT: punched
INFO: half gallon; Lid — one-piece steel with lock, red plastic handle; decal label; painted white inside; Bower Mfg. Co., Goshen, Ind.
GRADE: C

NO.: MBGB-33
NAME: Saving For New Wheels
HEIGHT: 10⅛"
SLOT: punched
INFO: half gallon; Lid — one-piece steel with lock, red plastic handle; decal label; painted white inside; Bower Mfg. Co., Goshen, Ind.
GRADE: C

Alcohol Bottle Banks

No.: ABGB-1
NAME: Mississippi Mud Beer
HEIGHT: 8¹³⁄₁₆"
SLOT: punched
INFO: Lid — black, tan aluminum, Mississippi Mud Black & Tan; Label — plastic bonded to glass; The Memphis Brewing Co., Memphis, Tenn., 1996, 1 Qt.
GRADE: B

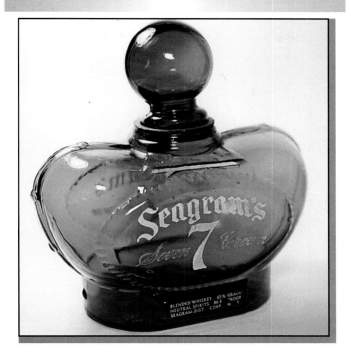

No.: ABGB-2
NAME: Seagrams 7 Crown Decanter
HEIGHT: 6¾"
SLOT: cut in glass
INFO: Lid — removable glass top; Seagram Dist. Corp., N.Y.
GRADE: D

No.: ABGB-3
NAME: Old Forester Display Bottle
HEIGHT: 19"
SLOT: cut in top
INFO: Lid — wooden; Old Forrester Kentucky Straight Bourbon Whiskey; Brown-Forman Distillers Corp., Louisville, Kentucky
GRADE: B

No.: ABGB-4
NAME: Kinsey Silver Display Bottle
HEIGHT: 13½"
SLOT: punched
INFO: Lid — black plastic; Kinsey Silver Blended Whiskey; Kinsey Distilling Co, Philadelphia, Pennsylvania
GRADE: B

No.: ABGB-5
NAME: Charter Oak Display Bottle
HEIGHT: 13½"
SLOT: punched
INFO: Lid — black plastic; Charter Oak Straight Bourbon Whisky; Continental Distilling Corp, Phila, Pa.
GRADE: B

NO.: ABGB-6
NAME: Haller's S-R-S Display Bottle
HEIGHT: 13½"
SLOT: punched
INFO: Lid — black plastic; Haller's S-R-S Blended Whiskey; W.A. Haller Co, Phila, Pa.
GRADE: B

NO.: ABGB-7
NAME: Christian Brothers Brandy Display Bottle
HEIGHT: 11¾"
SLOT: molded in glass
INFO: Lid — cream, red plastic; The Christian Bros. Brandy, Reedley, California; Fromm & Sichel Inc., N.Y., San Francisco, CA
GRADE: B

NO.: ABGB-8
NAME: Bourbon Supreme Display Bottle
HEIGHT: 12"
SLOT: punched
INFO: Lid — black slotted plastic
GRADE: B

NO.: ABGB-9
NAME: Samovar Vodka Bar Bottle For Tips
HEIGHT: 12³⁄₁₆"
SLOT: molded in base
INFO: Lid — white tin; Base — gold plastic, cash, tips, I.O.U. slots, holder for matches and pencil, bottom trap
GRADE: B

NO.: ABGB-10
NAME: Limbo Drummer on Oak Rum Bottle
HEIGHT: 10⅛"
SLOT: cut in plastic hat
INFO: Lid — metal lid under hat; Old Oak Rum, Limbo Drummer; Angostura Bitters; Trinidad, West Indies
GRADE: B

No.:   ABGB-11
NAME: Samovar Vodka Bar
         Bottle For Tips
HEIGHT: 12¼"
SLOT: molded in base
INFO: Lid — black plastic; Base
— black plastic, cash, tips,
I.O.U. slots, holder for matches
and pencil on chain in pencil
slot, bottom trap
GRADE: B

No.:   ABGB-12
NAME: Old Hickory Display Bottle
HEIGHT: 13⁹⁄₁₆"
SLOT: punched
INFO: Lid — black plastic; Old Hick-
ory Straight Bourbon Whisky; Old
Hickory Distributing Co., Philadel-
phia, Pa.
GRADE: B

No.:   ABGB-13
NAME: Bud Light
HEIGHT: 9"
SLOT: cut in glass back shoulder
INFO: Lid — metal still sealed;
Bud Light Beer
GRADE: A

RATING, GRADING	
A	To $15.00
B	$15.00 – 35.00
C	$35.00 – 75.00
D	$75.00 – 150.00
E	$150.00 – 300.00
F	$300.00 – 600.00
Rare	$600.00 – 1,000.00
Very Rare	negotiable

No.:   ABGB-14
NAME: Lauder's Scotch Display Bottle
HEIGHT: 12"
SLOT: cut in glass
INFO: Lid — metal sealed; Lauder's
Scotch Blended Scotch Whisky;
Archibald Lauder & Co Ltd., Glas-
gow, Scotland
GRADE: B

RATING, GRADING	
A	To $15.00
B	$15.00 – 35.00
C	$35.00 – 75.00
D	$75.00 – 150.00
E	$150.00 – 300.00
F	$300.00 – 600.00
Rare	$600.00 – 1,000.00
Very Rare	negotiable

NO.: ABGB-15
NAME: Seagrams V.O. Display Bottle
HEIGHT: 18½"
SLOT: punched
INFO: Lid — gold plastic; Seagram's V.O. Canadian Whisky; Joseph E. Seagram & Sons, Waterloo, Ontario, Canada; very heavy glass
GRADE: C

NO.: ABGB-16
NAME: Guckenheimer Display Bottle
HEIGHT: 14¹⁄₁₆"
SLOT: punched
INFO: Lid — gold tin; Guckenheimer American Whiskey; The American Distributing Co, Perkin, Ill, Sausalito, Ca; hole molded in bottom
GRADE: B

NO.: ABGB-17
NAME: Giant Calvert Reserve Display Bottle
HEIGHT: 27¾"
SLOT: routered in wood top
INFO: Lid — wooden top with cardboard collar; Front and back labels — Calvert Reserve Blended Whiskey; The Calvert Distilling Co., Baltimore, Md., Louisville, KY
GRADE: E

Giant Size Glass Banks

No.: GSGB-1
Name: Pig Change Holder
Height: 10¼"
Slot: punched
Info: Lid — cream colored plastic;
clear or green tint glass, 19½" long;
Rear — This Little Pig Went To Market,
Libbey Glass, 5 Gallon
Grade: D

No.: GSGB-2
Name: Mason Jar Change Holder
Height: 18"
Slot: non-slotted
Info: Lid — gold tin, 5¼" dia., green
glass; Mason's Patent, Nov. 30, 1858; eagle
molded on the back
Grade: E

No.: GSGB-3
Name: Mason Jar with Bail Handle Change Holder
Height: 14"
Slot: non-slotted
Info: Lid — white tin, 4¾" dia., clear glass;
Mason's Patent, Nov. 30, 1858; eagle molded on
the back
Grade: C

No.: GSGB-4
NAME: Auto Change Holder
HEIGHT: 10"
SLOT: non-slotted
INFO: Lid — black, gold with grill design, plain white tin, clear glass, 19½" long; Libbey Glass
GRADE: D

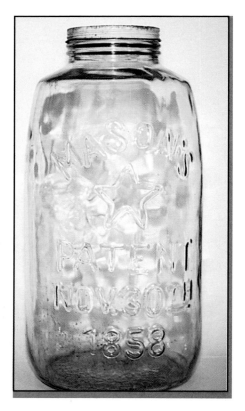

No.: GSGB-5
NAME: Amber Pig Change Holder
HEIGHT: 10"
SLOT: non-slotted
INFO: Lid — cork with nose design, 19" long, amber, blue tint, clear, smoke gray, green tint; Rear — This Little Pig Went To Market
GRADE: D

No.: GSGB-6
NAME: Mason Jar Change Holder
HEIGHT: 18½"
SLOT: non-slotted
INFO: Lid — white tin, 4¾" dia., clear glass; Mason's Patent, Nov. 30, 1858; eagle molded on back
GRADE: E

No.: GSGB-7
NAME: Hutchinson Coke Bottle Change Holder
HEIGHT: 20"
SLOT: open top
INFO: Georgia green glass, 1997; Property Of Coca-Cola Bottling Co.
GRADE: D

RATING, GRADING	
A	To $15.00
B	$15.00 – 35.00
C	$35.00 – 75.00
D	$75.00 – 150.00
E	$150.00 – 300.00
F	$300.00 – 600.00
Rare	$600.00 – 1,000.00
Very Rare	negotiable

No.: GSGB-8
NAME: Owl on Limb Change Holder
HEIGHT: 20¾"
SLOT: non-slotted
INFO: Lid — white tin; clear glass; Bottom — The Wise Old Owl
GRADE E

No.: GSGB-9
NAME: Amber Beer Bottle
HEIGHT: 20"
SLOT: punched
INFO: Lid — gold tin; amber glass
GRADE: C

NO.: GSGB-10
NAME: Coca-Cola Bottle
HEIGHT: 20"
SLOT: punched
INFO: Lid — tin litho;
green glass, 1962
GRADE D

NO.: GSGB-11
NAME: Eagle Milk Can
      Change Holder
HEIGHT: 18⅝"
SLOT: non-slotted
INFO: dark amber glass with
molded handles, stars, and
eagle; 1975 Owens Illinois
Glass; missing wooden lid
GRADE: D

NO.: GSGB-12
NAME: Glass Pig Change Holder
HEIGHT: 7½"
SLOT: non-slotted
INFO: clear glass pig with open nose
for cork closure; stands on concave rear
end; 12⅜" long; coil tail molded on top
GRADE: D

Artist-Made Glass Banks

NO.: AMGB-1
NAME: Fill-R-Up Quart Jar
HEIGHT: 6⅞"
SLOT: hand punched
INFO: Lid — two-piece canning jar, Harvest Mason jar; painted green with white flecks; hand painted by Tennessee artist
GRADE: B

NO.: AMGB-2
NAME: Homestead Fund Quart Jar
HEIGHT: 6⅞"
SLOT: hand punched
INFO: Lid — two-piece canning jar, Harvest Mason jar; painted green with white flecks; hand painted by Tennessee artist
GRADE: B

RATING, GRADING	
A	To $15.00
B	$15.00 – 35.00
C	$35.00 – 75.00
D	$75.00 – 150.00
E	$150.00 – 300.00
F	$300.00 – 600.00
Rare	$600.00 – 1,000.00
Very Rare	negotiable

NO.: AMGB-3
NAME: Po Folk's Fund Quart Jar
HEIGHT: 6⅞"
SLOT: hand punched
INFO: Lid — two-piece canning jar, Harvest Mason jar; painted green with white flecks; hand painted by Tennessee artist
GRADE: B

NO.: AMGB-5
NAME: Fill-R-Up Gallon Jug
HEIGHT: 11⅝"
SLOT: hand punched
INFO: Lid — tin; painted green with white flecks; hand painted by Tennessee artist
GRADE: B

NO.: AMGB-4
NAME: Farm Aid Gallon Jug
HEIGHT: 11⅝"
SLOT: hand punched
INFO: Lid — tin; painted green with white flecks; hand painted by Tennessee artist
GRADE: B

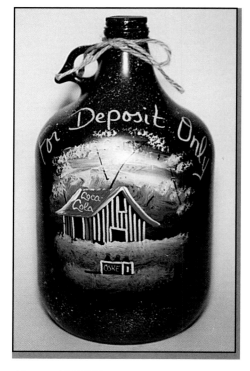

NO.: AMGB-6
NAME: Grump Quart Jar
HEIGHT: 7"
SLOT: hand punched
INFO: Lid — white tin, clear glass; paper label with stocking girl face glued on by Helen
GRADE: A

NO.: AMGB-7
NAME: For Deposit Only Gallon Jug
HEIGHT: 11⅝"
SLOT: hand punched
INFO: Lid — tin; painted green with white flecks; hand painted by Tennessee artist
GRADE: B

No.:   AMGB-8
NAME: Gamblin Fund
HEIGHT: 11⅝"
SLOT: hand punched
INFO: Lid — tin; painted blue with white flecks; hand painted by Tennessee artist
GRADE: B

No.:   AMGB-9
NAME: Choo-Choo Change
HEIGHT: 11⅝"
SLOT: hand punched
INFO: Lid — tin; painted green with white flecks; hand painted by Tennessee artist
GRADE: B

No.:   AMGB-10
NAME: Ball Perfect Mason
HEIGHT 7⅜"
SLOT: punched
INFO: Lid — oak with metal slotted insert; blue green glass
GRADE: B

No.:   AMGB-11
NAME: Atlas Mason Patent
HEIGHT: 7¼"
SLOT: punched
INFO: Lid — oak with metal slotted insert; green glass
GRADE: B

No.: AMGB-12
NAME: Alfred E. Newman Gallon Jug
HEIGHT: 11¾"
SLOT: hand punched
INFO: Lid — white tin; Alfred E. Newman face stenciled on glass
GRADE: B

No.: AMGB-13
NAME: Casino Fund
HEIGHT: 6⅝"
SLOT: punched or cut
INFO: Lid — two-piece lid with cut slot; glass is a golden harvest Mason
GRADE: A

No.: AMGB-14
NAME: Millennium Bee Hive
HEIGHT: 4¼"
SLOT: punched
INFO: edition of nine banks; Lid — white tin; nine of these banks were made December 31, 1999, as the last glass bank of the past millennium; used old jars, machine punched with new paper labels; Reynolds Toys
GRADE: C

See page 7 for price ranges.

Lid & Label Variations

Koop Jar Banks

These nine Koops jar banks made by Rolland Mills Inc. of Chicago show variations of lids and labels.

Rare Bank Bottles

87

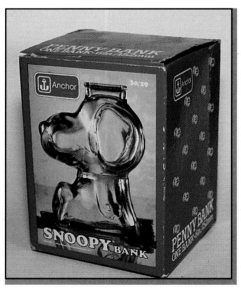

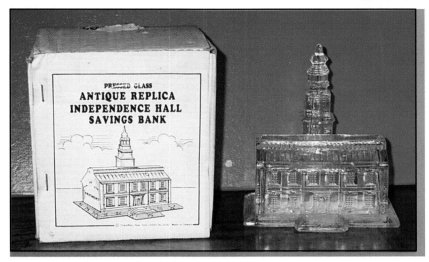

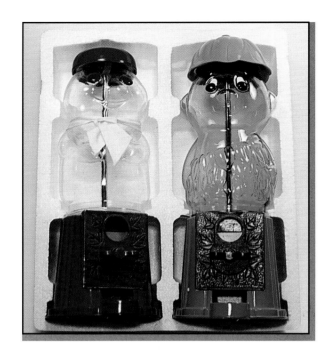

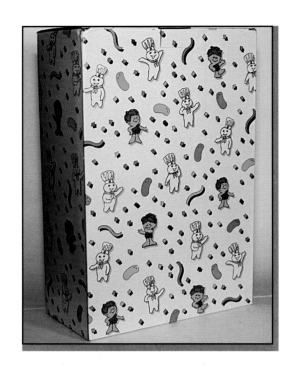

Glass Banks with Rare Labels

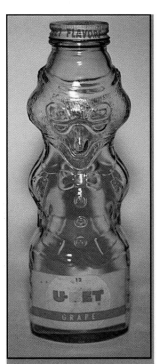

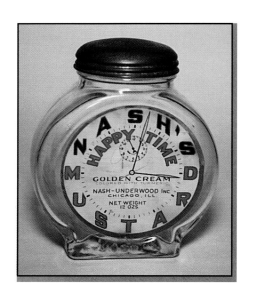

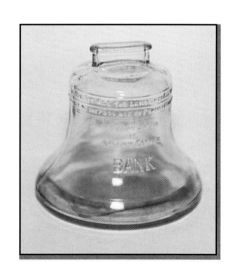

LID & LABEL VARIATIONS – GLASS BANKS WITH RARE LABELS

94

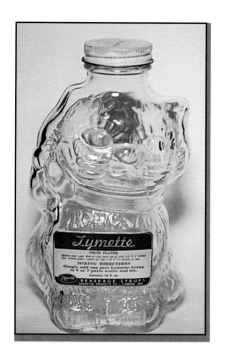

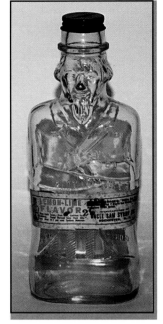

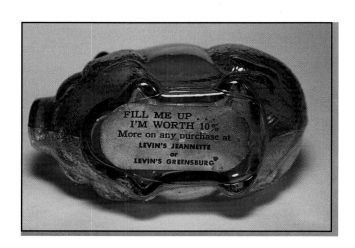

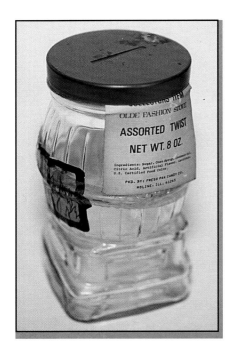

Reproduction lids with names misspelled.

99

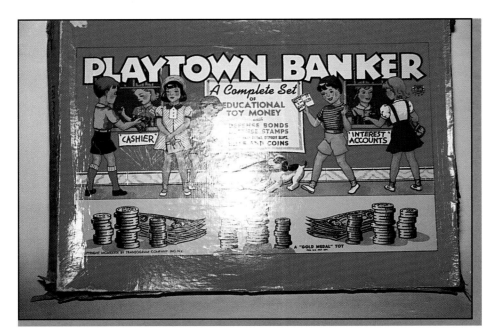

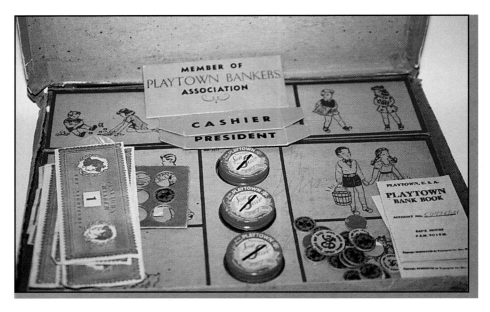

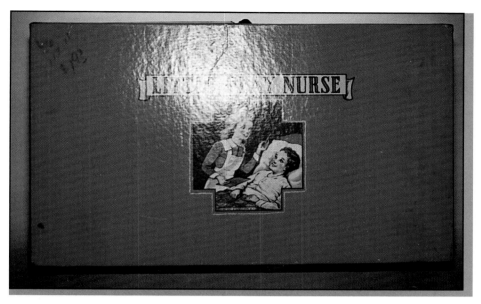

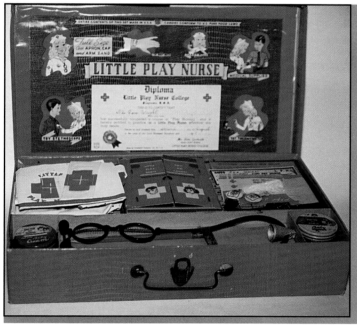

Inverted Bottle Banks

Bottles with Lids on the Bottom

See page 7 for price ranges.

No.: IGB-1
NAME: Clear Glass Baseball
HEIGHT: 3⁹⁄₁₆"
SLOT: punched
INFO: Lid — gold tin; clear glass
GRADE: B

No.: IGB-2
NAME: Baseball
HEIGHT: 3¼"
SLOT: punched
INFO: Lid — black tin, Patent Applied For, round black plastic base; painted white inside glass
GRADE: B

No.: IGB-3
NAME: Pittsburgh Pirates United Cerebral Palsy
HEIGHT: 3⅜"
SLOT: punched
INFO: Lid — gold tin, round black plastic base; painted white inside glass
GRADE: C

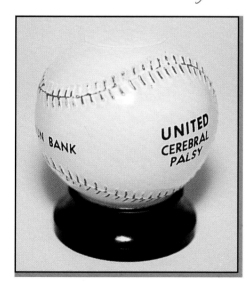

No.: IGB-4
NAME: Home Run Bank United Cerebral Palsy
HEIGHT: 3½"
SLOT: punched
INFO: Lid — gold tin, round black plastic base; painted white inside glass
GRADE: C

No.: IGB-5
NAME: Mobil Flying Horse Indian Head
HEIGHT: 3½"
SLOT: punched
INFO: Lid — black tin, round black plastic base; painted white inside glass
GRADE: C

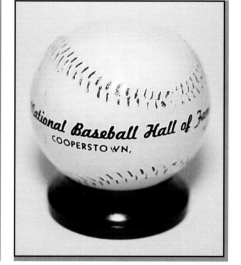

No.: IGB-6
NAME: National Baseball Hall of Fame and Museum, Cooperstown, N.Y.
HEIGHT: 3½"
SLOT: punched
INFO: Lid — black tin, round black plastic base; painted white inside glass
GRADE: D

NO.: IGB-7
NAME: Custard Glass Baseball
HEIGHT: 3½"
SLOT: punched
INFO: Lid — gold tin, round black plastic base
GRADE: D

NO.: IGB-8
NAME: Knoxville Smokies Mobil Flying Horse
HEIGHT: 3⁹⁄₁₆"
SLOT: punched
INFO: Lid — black tin, Patent Applied For, Neffelfinger Publications, N.Y.; painted white inside glass
GRADE: D

NO.: IGB-9
NAME: State Bank of Long Beach
HEIGHT: 3½"
SLOT: punched
INFO: Lid — black tin, round black plastic base; painted white inside glass
GRADE: C

NO.: IGB-10
NAME: Morrow Milling Co, Carthage, MO
HEIGHT: 3⁷⁄₁₆"
SLOT: punched
INFO: Lid — black tin, Patent Applied For; painted white inside glass
GRADE: D

NO.: IGB-11
NAME: Mobil Flying Horse, Tiger baseball on square base
HEIGHT: 3½"
SLOT: punched
INFO: Lid — black tin, Koster Dana-Barrell Inc., 30 Broad St, New York 4, N.Y.; rare square black plastic base; painted white inside glass
GRADE: F

NO.: IGB-12
NAME: St. Louis Cardinals
HEIGHT: 3½"
SLOT: punched
INFO: Lid — black tin, round black plastic base; painted white inside glass
GRADE: D

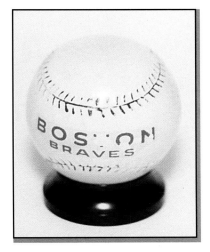

No.:   IGB-13
Name: Philadelphia A's
Height: 3½"
Slot: punched
Info: Lid — black tin, round black plastic base; painted white inside glass
Grade: D

No.:   IGB-14
Name: Boston Braves
Height: 3½"
Slot: punched
Info: Lid — black tin, round black plastic base; painted white inside glass
Grade: D

No.:   IGB-15
Name: American LIfe and Casualty Co
Height: 3½"
Slot: punched
Info: Lid — black tin, round black plastic base; painted white inside glass
Grade: D

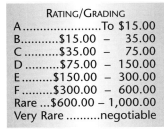

RATING/GRADING	
A	To $15.00
B	$15.00 – 35.00
C	$35.00 – 75.00
D	$75.00 – 150.00
E	$150.00 – 300.00
F	$300.00 – 600.00
Rare	$600.00 – 1,000.00
Very Rare	negotiable

No.:   IGB-16
Name: Gullistan Rugs & Carpets
Height: 3½"
Slot: punched
Info: Lid — black tin, round black plastic base; painted white inside glass
Grade: D

No.:   IGB-17
Name: McElreath Beverage Co.
Height: 3½"
Slot: punched
Info: Lid — black tin, round black plastic base; painted white inside glass
Grade: D

No.:   IGB-18
Name: Ru-Ber-Oid
Height: 3½"
Slot: punched
Info: Lid — black tin, round black plastic base; painted white inside glass
Grade: D

No.: IGB-19
NAME: Giants
HEIGHT: 3½"
SLOT: punched
INFO: Lid — black tin, round black plastic base; painted white inside glass
GRADE: D

No.: IGB-20
NAME: Weather Bird Shoes
HEIGHT: 3½"
SLOT: punched
INFO: Lid — black tin, round black plastic base; painted white inside glass
GRADE: D

No.: IGB-21
NAME: Savings Up to $5000
HEIGHT: 3½"
SLOT: punched
INFO: Lid — black tin, round black plastic base; painted white inside glass
GRADE: D

No.: IGB-22
NAME: Snow Crest Type Bear with Bottom Opening
HEIGHT: 6⅞"
SLOT: converted and non-slotted
INFO: Lid — plastic plug; Copyright 1980, B. Shackman & Co.
GRADE: D

No.: IGB-23
NAME: Koala Bear
HEIGHT: 6¼"
SLOT: converted and non-slotted
INFO: Lid — black or blue plastic; San Diego Zoo
GRADE: C

No.: IGB-24
NAME: Santa Head
HEIGHT: 6½"
SLOT: converted and non-slotted
INFO: Lid — tin with paper label, contained candy, Argentina; usually found painted on outside
GRADE: D

NO.: IGB-25
NAME: Beehive Bank, World's Fair 1893
HEIGHT: 2⅞"
SLOT: molded in glass
INFO: Lid — plain tin screws on (this one is held on with wax); says How Doth The Little Busy with picture of bee entering hive
GRADE: E

NO.: IGB-26
NAME: Santa with Pack
HEIGHT: 8¼"
SLOT: converted and non-slotted
INFO: Lid — gold tin; painted on outside of glass; from Argentina
GRADE: D

RATING/GRADING	
A	To $15.00
B	$15.00 – 35.00
C	$35.00 – 75.00
D	$75.00 – 150.00
E	$150.00 – 300.00
F	$300.00 – 600.00
Rare	$600.00 – 1,000.00
Very Rare	negotiable

NO.: IGB-27
NAME: Inverted Owl Bank
HEIGHT: 4⅝"
SLOT: punched and non-slotted
INFO: Lid — white tin; colors found — green, clear, cobalt blue, peach
GRADE: B

Upside Downs

These banks will stand on their bottoms or their tops

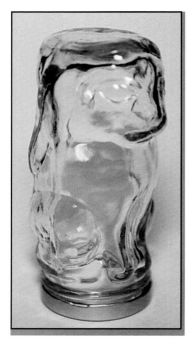

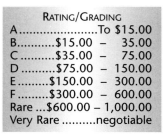

No.:　UD-1
NAME: Rabbit
HEIGHT: 4¾"
SLOT:　converted and non-slotted
INFO:　Lid — twist-on tin; The
Frank Tea & Spice Co., Cinn.,
Ohio
GRADE: E

No.:　UD-2
NAME: Parrot
HEIGHT: 4¾"
SLOT:　converted and non-slotted
INFO:　Lid — twist-on tin; The Frank
Tea & Spice Co., Cinn., Ohio
GRADE: E

No.:　UD-3
NAME: Dog
HEIGHT: 4¾"
SLOT:　converted and non-slotted
INFO:　Lid — twist-on tin; The
Frank Tea & Spice Co., Cinn.,
Ohio
GRADE: E

No.:　UD-4
NAME: Monkey
HEIGHT: 4¾"
SLOT:　converted and non-slotted
INFO:　Lid — twist-on tin; The
Frank Tea & Spice Co., Cinn.,
Ohio
GRADE: E

No.: UD-5
NAME: Owl
HEIGHT: 4¾"
SLOT: converted and non-slotted
INFO: Lid — twist-on tin; The Frank Tea & Spice Co., Cinn., Ohio
GRADE: E

No.: UD-6
NAME: Cat
HEIGHT: 4¾"
SLOT: converted and non-slotted
INFO: Lid — twist-on tin; The Frank Tea & Spice Co., Cinn., Ohio
GRADE: E

No.: UD-8
NAME: Jumbo Peanut Butter
HEIGHT: 3⅜"
SLOT: punched
INFO: Lid — litho tin, Jumbo Peanut Butter, 3½ ozs. net; Write For New Peanut Butter Recipes; The Frank Tea & Spice Co., Cinn., O.; clear glass
GRADE: Very Rare

No.: UD-7
NAME: Jumbo Peanut Butter
Height: 3⅜"
SLOT: punched
INFO: Lid — litho tin, Jumbo Peanut Butter, 3½ ozs. net; Write For New Peanut Butter Recipes; The Frank Tea & Spice Co., Cinn. O.; green glass
GRADE: Very Rare

109

All Glass Banks

NO.: AG-1
NAME: Carnival Glass Pig
HEIGHT: 4⅞"
SLOT: raised slot
INFO: Anchor Hocking; also found in clear glass
GRADE: A

NO.: AG-2
NAME: Carnival Glass Pig
HEIGHT: 3"
SLOT: raised slot
INFO: Anchor Hocking; also found in clear glass; Bottom labels found — Leving's Jeannette, Provident Fed Savings
GRADE: A

NO.: AG-3
NAME: Save With Marathon, The Ohio Oil Co.
HEIGHT: 3"
SLOT: raised slot
INFO: carnival glass
GRADE: C

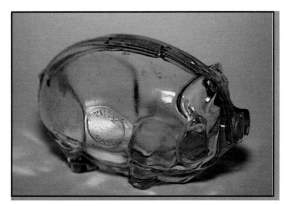

NO.: AG-4
NAME: Piggy
HEIGHT: 2¾"
SLOT: molded in split area
INFO: clear glass; piggy bank in circle on both sides; split to open
GRADE: C

RATING/GRADING	
A	To $15.00
B	$15.00 – 35.00
C	$35.00 – 75.00
D	$75.00 – 150.00
E	$150.00 – 300.00
F	$300.00 – 600.00
Rare	$600.00 – 1,000.00
Very Rare	negotiable

No.: AG-5
NAME: Piggy Bank
HEIGHT: 3¾"
SLOT: raised arch slot
INFO: piggy bank on both sides
GRADE: amber: C; cobalt: C; clear: D

No.: AG-6
NAME: Taiwan Hobnail Pig
HEIGHT: 3⅛"
SLOT: cut slot and non-cut slot
INFO: round open cork nose; green, milk, amber, blue
GRADE: C

No.: AG-7
NAME: Short Nose S-Tail Pig
HEIGHT: 3⅜"
SLOT: cut slot
INFO: hobnail clear glass, upside down heart nose, tail in letter "S" shape
GRADE: D

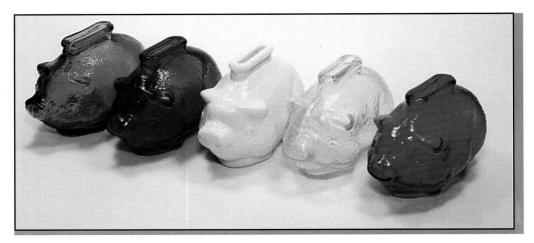

No.:   AG-8
NAME: Taiwan Repro Pig
HEIGHT: 2⅞"
SLOT: raised
INFO: slot is longer than the original bank; green, blue, milk, pink, red; ROC paper label
GRADE: A

No.:   AG-9
NAME: Taiwan Advertising Repro Coca-Cola Pig
HEIGHT: 2⅞"
SLOT: raised
INFO: found with several screened logos on blue glass and milk glass
GRADE: B

No.:   AG-10
NAME: Large Rabbit with Grass
HEIGHT: 5"
SLOT: raised
INFO: usually found in carnival glass; this one is factory painted
GRADE: F

No.:   AG-11
NAME: Large Rabbit without Grass
HEIGHT: 4¼"
SLOT: raised
INFO: carnival glass
GRADE: F

No.:   AG-12
NAME: Small Rabbit with Grass
HEIGHT: 3⅛"
SLOT: raised
INFO: carnival glass
GRADE: E

No.:   AG-13
NAME: Small Rabbit without Grass
HEIGHT: 2⅞"
SLOT: raised
INFO: carnival glass
GRADE: E

No.:   AG-14
NAME: Cork Nose Fish
HEIGHT: 3"
SLOT: cut in top
INFO: green, blue, purple, may be others
GRADE: C

No.:   AG-15
NAME: Half Hobnail Pig
HEIGHT: 3⅜"
SLOT: cut in top
INFO: dark smoke gray; front half hobnail pattern, back half smooth with no tail; round cork nose
GRADE: D

No.:   AG-16
NAME: Long Closed Nose Pig
HEIGHT: 3½"
SLOT: raised
INFO: 4¾" long; green, medium blue
GRADE: C

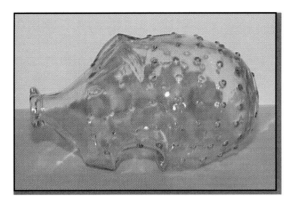

No.: AG-17
NAME: Long Upside-down Heart Nose Pig
HEIGHT: 3¼"
SLOT: cut in top
INFO: sometimes called a hedgehog; longer than the colored glass versions
GRADE: C

No.: AG-18
NAME: Gold-plated Pig
HEIGHT: 3"
SLOT: raised
INFO: Emblem — Meramec Caverns, Jesse James, Hide Out, MO
GRADE: C

No.: AG-19
NAME: Belgium Pig
HEIGHT: 3¹⁵⁄₁₆"
SLOT: raised
INFO: clear glass; Under front legs — Container Made in Belgium
GRADE: C

No.: AG-20
NAME: Taiwan Small Plain Pig
HEIGHT: 3½"
SLOT: raised
INFO: clear glass, very little detail or definition; closed nose
GRADE: B

No.: AG-21
NAME: "Schwein gehabt" Pig
HEIGHT: 4"
SLOT: raised
INFO: clear glass
GRADE: C

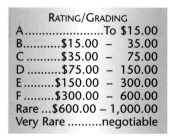

RATING/GRADING	
A	To $15.00
B	$15.00 – 35.00
C	$35.00 – 75.00
D	$75.00 – 150.00
E	$150.00 – 300.00
F	$300.00 – 600.00
Rare	$600.00 – 1,000.00
Very Rare	negotiable

NO.: AG-22
NAME: Taiwan Large Plain Pig
HEIGHT: 4¼"
SLOT: raised
INFO: clear glass, very little detail or definition; closed nose
GRADE: B

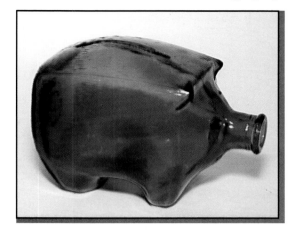

NO.: AG-23
NAME: Finland Pig
HEIGHT: 3⁵⁄₁₆"
SLOT: cut in top
INFO: square design with round open nose; horizontal small hair line design in glass; Box — Riihimaki Finland; amber glass; blue glass
GRADE: C

NO.: AG-24
NAME: Irma Pig
HEIGHT: 3¼"
SLOT: cut in top
INFO: Irma name in bottom, clear glass
GRADE: C

NO.: AG-25
NAME: Pig, cobalt
HEIGHT: 4⅞"
SLOT: raised
INFO: heavy cobalt blue, tall, straight horizontal line
GRADE: D

NO.: AG-26
NAME: Pig, opaque
HEIGHT: 4⅞"
SLOT: raised
INFO: colors flashed over clear glass; no color on bottom; blue, yellow, red, green, maybe others
GRADE: B

No.: AG-27
NAME: Short Pig
HEIGHT: 3¹⁵/₁₆"
SLOT: raised
INFO: Under front legs — Container Made in Belgium; decal labels on both sides, Germany on back; clear glass
GRADE: C

No.: AG-28
NAME: Pig, transparent
HEIGHT: 4⅞"
SLOT: raised
INFO: color flashed over clear glass, no color on bottom; green, yellow, blue, red, orange, maybe others
GRADE: B

No.: AG-29
NAME: Hobnail Pig
HEIGHT: 3⁵/₁₆"
SLOT: cut and non-cut
INFO: upside-down heart nose; green, cobalt, amber, clear, maybe others
GRADE: C

RATING/GRADING	
A	To $15.00
B	$15.00 – 35.00
C	$35.00 – 75.00
D	$75.00 – 150.00
E	$150.00 – 300.00
F	$300.00 – 600.00
Rare	$600.00 – 1,000.00
Very Rare	negotiable

No.: AG-30
NAME: Pig
HEIGHT: 4⅞"
SLOT: cut in top
INFO: large clear glass pig with cork nose; hammered design in glass, thick heavy glass
GRADE: D

NO.: AG-31
NAME: Eyelash Pig
HEIGHT: 4¾"
SLOT: raised
INFO: smoke, colonial brown; Libbey
Glass, Toledo, Ohio
GRADE: B

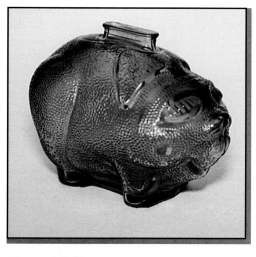

NO.: AG-33
NAME: Pig with
       Nose Up
HEIGHT: 3¾"
SLOT: cut in top
INFO: cobalt blue
GRADE: D

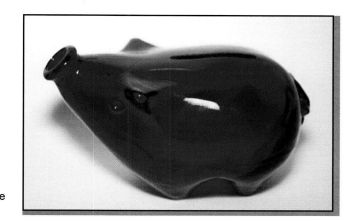

NO.: AG-32
NAME: The Water Saver Speed Queen Pig
HEIGHT: 4⅝"
SLOT: raised
INFO: label screened on bottom, The Water
Saver, Speed Queen, smoke glass
GRADE: C

NO.: AG-34
NAME: Teddy Bear Bow Tie
HEIGHT: 6³⁄₁₆"
SLOT: raised
INFO: pink, clear
GRADE: D

No.: AG-35
Name: Chadwick-Miller Pig
Height: 4³⁄₁₆"
Slot: non-slotted
Info: Box — Chadwick-Miller Piggy Bank, see-through glass, removable coke snout; Chadwick-Miller Inc, Boston, Mass., Taiwan 1974
Grade: D

No.: AG-36
Name: Niagara Falls Pig
Height: 4⅞"
Slot: raised
Info: factory painted souvenir, owner marked it Aug 22, 1962
Grade: B

No.: AG-37
Name: Liberty Bell
Height: 3¾"
Slot: raised, short slot
Info: A Penny Saved Is a Penny Earned; no horizontal lines molded between lines of lettering; no molded crack, clear glass
Grade: A

No.: AG-38
Name: Liberty Bell
Height: 3¾"
Slot: raised, short slot
Info: A Penny Saved Is a Penny Earned; with horizontal lines molded between lines of lettering; no molded crack, clear or carnival glass
Grade: A

No.: AG-39
Name: Liberty Bell
Height: 3¾"
Slot: raised, short slot
Info: clear glass; with red, white, and blue
horizontal painted lines; no molded crack
Grade: B

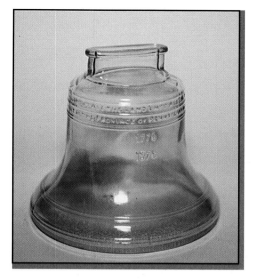

No.: AG-40
Name: Liberty Bell 1776 – 1976
Height: 3¾"
Slot: raised, long slot
Info: molded crack, carnival glass
Grade: A

See page 7 for price ranges.

No.: AG-41
Name: Blue Liberty Bell 1776 – 1976
Height: 3¾"
Slot: raised, long slot
Info: colored blue inside glass
Grade: B

No.: AG-42
Name: Liberty Bell on Wooden Base
Height: 4½"
Slot: raised, long slot
Info: carnival glass; Base — Niagra Falls N.Y., 1776 – Liberty
Bell Bank – 1976; found marked for other locations as souvenirs
Grade: B

No.:   AG-43
Name: Liberty Bell
Height: 3¾"
Slot: raised, long slot
Info: amber glass, Anchor Hocking
Grade: E

No.:   AG-44
Name: Liberty Bell Guardian Federal Savings &
        Loan
Height: 3¾"
Slot: raised, short slot
Info: carnival glass
Grade: C

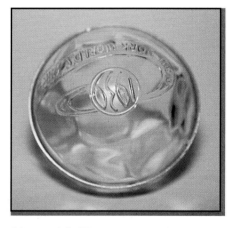

No.:   AG-45
Name: Small Liberty Bell
Height: 2⅝"
Slot: raised
Info: clear glass, molded crack;
Proclaim Liberty Throughout All the
Land Unto All the Inhabitants Thereof
Grade: F

No.:   AG-46
Name: 1939 World's Fair Ball
Height: 2⅞"
Slot: molded-in seam
Info: clear glass; split to open type
Grade: D

No.:   AG-47
Name: Upside-down 1939 World's Fair
        Ball
Height: 2⅞"
Slot: molded-in seam
Info: clear glass; split to open type
Grade: Rare

RATING/GRADING	
A	To $15.00
B	$15.00 – 35.00
C	$35.00 – 75.00
D	$75.00 – 150.00
E	$150.00 – 300.00
F	$300.00 – 600.00
Rare	$600.00 – 1,000.00
Very Rare	negotiable

NO.: AG-48
NAME: Lucky Barrel
HEIGHT: 4⅜"
SLOT: raised
INFO: clear glass, Lucky Bank front and back
GRADE: B

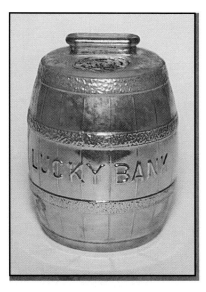

NO.: AG-49
NAME: Lucky Barrel, carnival glass
HEIGHT: 4⅜"
SLOT: raised
INFO: Lucky Bank front and back
GRADE: C

NO.: AG-50
NAME: Barrel
HEIGHT: 4½"
SLOT: raised
INFO: clear glass, Barrel Bank front and back; carnival glass version may exist
GRADE: B

NO.: AG-51
NAME: Treasure Chest Trunk
HEIGHT: 3½"
SLOT: raised
INFO: clear glass, Treasure Chest front and back; variation may exist
GRADE: C

NO.: AG-52
NAME: Thatched Roof Cottage
HEIGHT: 4⅛"
SLOT: raised
INFO: probably English; Back — two windows; Sides — one window each
GRADE: E

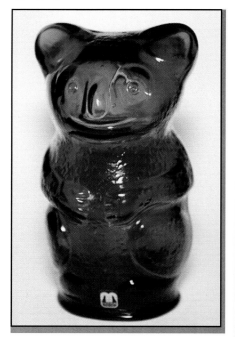

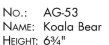

No.: AG-53
NAME: Koala Bear
HEIGHT: 6¾"
SLOT: molded in back of neck
INFO: amber glass; Label — Cascade England
GRADE: D

No.: AG-54
NAME: Wheaton Uncle Sam
HEIGHT: 6"
SLOT: raised
INFO: green, blue; Bottom — Wheaton N.J.
GRADE: C

No.: AG-55
NAME: Wheaton Federal Savings Vault
HEIGHT: 6"
SLOT: raised
INFO: green, blue, ruby; Bottom — Wheaton N.J.
GRADE: C, ruby: E

No.: AG-56
NAME: Ranger Joe Barrel
HEIGHT: 4½"
SLOT: raised
INFO: clear glass
GRADE: D

No.: AG-57
NAME: Wheaton Flint Glass 1888 Factory
HEIGHT: 6"
SLOT: raised
INFO: light green, green, blue, clear in 1999; Back — T.C. Wheaton Co. Flint Glass Manufactures Founded 1888; Bottom — Wheaton N.J.
GRADE: C

RATING/GRADING	
A	To $15.00
B	$15.00 – 35.00
C	$35.00 – 75.00
D	$75.00 – 150.00
E	$150.00 – 300.00
F	$300.00 – 600.00
Rare	$600.00 – 1,000.00
Very Rare	negotiable

NO.: AG-58
NAME: Wheaton Pot Belly Stove
HEIGHT: 6"
SLOT: raised
INFO: blue, green, ruby
GRADE: C, ruby: E

NO.: AG-59
NAME: Wheaton Indian Chief
HEIGHT: 6"
SLOT: raised
INFO: blue, green
GRADE: C

NO.: AG-60
NAME: Wheaton 1st National Bank
HEIGHT: 6"
SLOT: raised
INFO: blue, green, ruby
GRADE: C, ruby: E

NO.: AG-61
NAME: Lenape Indian, 1980
HEIGHT: 6"
SLOT: raised
INFO: ruby glass; Bottom — Lenape
State Bank, picture of a tepee
GRADE: D

NO.: AG-62
NAME: Lenape Indian, 1981
HEIGHT: 6"
SLOT: raised
INFO: amber glass; Bottom — Lenape
State Bank, picture of a tepee
GRADE: D

No.:   AG-63
NAME: Lenape Indian, 1982
HEIGHT: 6"
SLOT: raised
INFO: dark green glass; Bottom —
Lenape State Bank, picture of a tepee
GRADE: D

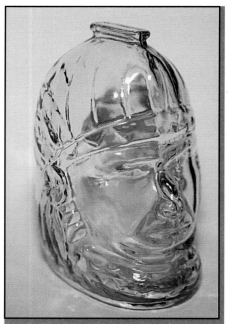

No.:   AG-64
NAME: Lenape Indian, 1983
HEIGHT: 6"
SLOT: raised
INFO: clear glass; Bottom — Lenape
State Bank, picture of a tepee
GRADE: E

No.:   AG-65
NAME: Lenape Indian, 1984
HEIGHT: 6"
SLOT: raised
INFO: light green glass; Bottom — Lenape
State Bank, picture of a tepee
GRADE: D

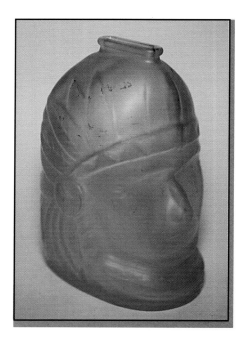

No.:   AG-66
NAME: Lenape Indian, 1985
HEIGHT: 6"
SLOT: raised
INFO: frosted clear glass; Bottom — Lenape
State Bank, picture of a tepee
GRADE: D

No.:   AG-67
NAME: Wheaton Bobby Hat, Uncle Sam
HEIGHT: 6"
SLOT: raised
INFO: blue, green; probably Uncle Sam that
did not completely fill mold in production; many
have been found
GRADE: D

No.: AG-69
NAME: World Globe
HEIGHT: 4⅛"
SLOT: raised
INFO: carnival glass;
horizontal lined base
GRADE: C

No.: AG-68
NAME: World Globe
HEIGHT: 4⅛"
SLOT: raised
INFO: clear glass; horizontal lined base
GRADE: B

RATING/GRADING	
A	To $15.00
B	$15.00 – 35.00
C	$35.00 – 75.00
D	$75.00 – 150.00
E	$150.00 – 300.00
F	$300.00 – 600.00
Rare	$600.00 – 1,000.00
Very Rare	negotiable

No.: AG-70
NAME: Large Float bank
HEIGHT: 4¼"
SLOT: raised
INFO: green glass sitting on clear coaster, height without coaster; other sizes and colors exist
GRADE: C

No.: AG-71
NAME: World Globe
HEIGHT: 4⅛"
SLOT: raised
INFO: clear glass, six flutes in base, BANK
GRADE: B; amber: E

No.: AG-72
NAME: World Globe
HEIGHT: 4⅛"
SLOT: raised
INFO: clear glass sil-
vered inside, six flutes
in base, BANK
GRADE: C

No.: AG-73
Name: Eagle-Gazette Globe
Height: 4⅛"
Slot: raised
Info: clear glass; 1809 – 1947, Lancaster, Ohio, Eagle-Gazette; horizontal lined base
Grade: D

No.: AG-74
Name: Two-piece Ball on Base
Height: 3⅞"
Slot: raised
Info: clear glass, Label — Cent-Enary Seal, Coin Collector; labels held the bank together
Grade: E

No.: AG-75
Name: Major Gas Miniature Fish Bowl
Height: 2¼"
Slot: molded in top
Info: clear glass; Decal label — Save With Major Gas
Grade: Rare

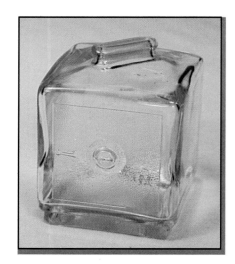

No.: AG-76
Name: Glass Safe with Diagonal Slot
Height: 3½"
Slot: raised
Info: clear glass
Grade: F

No.: AG-77
Name: Ornate Vault
Height: 4"
Slot: molded in back
Info: clear glass; Savings Bank on doors
Grade: E

RATING/GRADING	
A.........................To $15.00	
B...........$15.00 – 35.00	
C..........$35.00 – 75.00	
D..........$75.00 – 150.00	
E.........$150.00 – 300.00	
F.........$300.00 – 600.00	
Rare ...$600.00 – 1,000.00	
Very Rare ....negotiable	

No.: AG-78
Name: Save For Santa
Height: 5¾"
Slot: raised
Info: clear glass; Save For Santa on bottom edge of coat
Grade: F

No.: AG-79
Name: Radio
Height: 3⅛"
Slot: raised arched slot
Info: clear glass; Radio Bank on front top and large letters on back
Grade: C

No.: AG-80
Name: Pittsburgh Paints House
Height: 2¾"
Slot: molded-in seam
Info: clear glass split-to-open type; Save With Pittsburgh Paints, Smooth As Glass; Nature's Colors in Lasting Beauty
Grade: C

No.: AG-81
Name: Pittsburgh Paints House
Height: 2¾"
Slot: molded-in seam
Info: split-to-open type; glass seems to be stained a very dark blue, factory done
Grade: E

No.: AG-82
Name: Westmoreland Mustard Brick House
Height: 3⅞"
Slot: punch out in chimney
Info: milk glass painted gold; Paper label on bottom — Prepared Mustard, Westmoreland Specialty Co., Grapeville, Pa.
Grade: D

NO.: AG-83
NAME: Canadian Log Cabin Moutarde
HEIGHT: 3⅞"
SLOT: punch out in chimney
INFO: milk glass painted gold; Paper label on bottom — Moutarde, S.H. Ewing & Sons, Montreal
GRADE: D

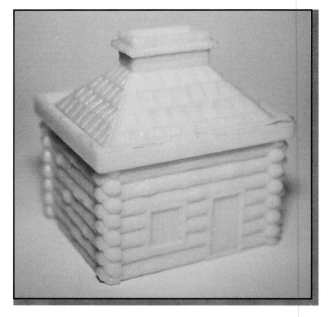

NO.: AG-84
NAME: Westmoreland Mustard Log Cabin
HEIGHT: 3⅞"
SLOT: punch out in chimney
INFO: milk glass painted gold; paper label as on AG-81; Paper label — to seal melt paraffin wax around top edge, knock out piece of glass from underside
GRADE: D

NO.: AG-85
NAME: Coal and Coke Oven
HEIGHT: 4⅝"
SLOT: raised
INFO: light green, dark green, amber; Coal and Coke Museum, Pennsylvania, 1843 – 1969
GRADE: C

NO.: AG-86
NAME: Kroger Building
HEIGHT: 3⅞"
SLOT: raised
INFO: clear glass; KROGER on vertical markees; Live Better for Less
GRADE: Rare

No.: AG-87
Name: Be Wise Owl
Height: 6⅞"
Slot: raised
Info: carnival glass, some very light and some very dark; BE WISE on base front
Grade: C

No.: AG-88
Name: Be Wise Owl
Height: 6⅞"
Slot: raised
Info: dark amber glass; Anchor Hocking
Grade: E

No.: AG-89
Name: Royal Ruby Owl
Height: 7"
Slot: raised
Info: ruby glass; Bottom Royal Ruby, Anchor Glass
Grade: Rare

No.: AG-90
Name: Two-piece Elephant
Height: 3⅞"
Slot: raised
Info: clear glass
Grade: E

RATING/GRADING	
A	To $15.00
B	$15.00 – 35.00
C	$35.00 – 75.00
D	$75.00 – 150.00
E	$150.00 – 300.00
F	$300.00 – 600.00
Rare	$600.00 – 1,000.00
Very Rare	negotiable

No.: AG-91
Name: Pirate Chest
Height: 4¾"
Slot: raised
Info: dark amber glass
Grade: A

NO.: AG-92
NAME: Garfield
HEIGHT: 7½"
SLOT: raised
INFO: clear glass; Anchor Hocking
GRADE: A

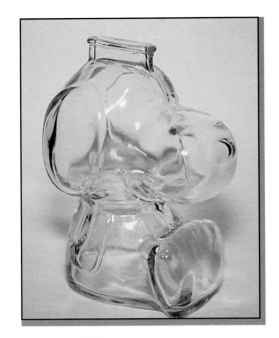

NO.: AG-93
NAME: Snoopy
HEIGHT: 6"
SLOT: raised
INFO: clear glass; Anchor Hocking
GRADE: A

NO.: AG-94
NAME: Snoopy
HEIGHT: 6"
SLOT: raised
INFO: clear glass; ears, arms, and name etched on front of feet, ETHEL
GRADE: B

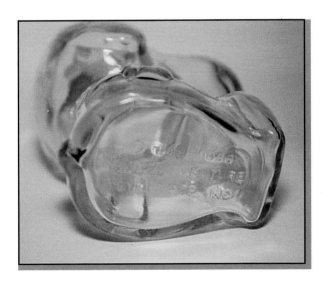

NO.: AG-95
NAME: United Feature Syndicate Snoopy
HEIGHT: 6"
SLOT: raised
INFO: clear glass; Bottom — raised letters, 1958 – 1966, United Feature Syndicate, Inc.
GRADE: C

No.: AG-96
Name: Wise Old Owl with
Graduation Hat
Height: 6¼"
Slot: raised
Info: clear glass; white plastic grad-
uation hat with string tassel; Bottom —
Wise Old Owl
Grade: C

No.: AG-97
Name: Wise Old Owl
Height: 6⅜"
Slot: raised
Info: clear glass; tan rubber stopper, held
various liquid products
Grade: B

No.: AG-98
Name: Wise Old Owl
Height: 6¼"
Slot: raised
Info: clear glass; moving doll eyes,
questionable as to manufacture
Grade: B

No.: AG-99
Name: Wise Old Owl
Height: 6¼"
Slot: raised
Info: smoke, amber brown, clear, clear
frosted; Bottom — Wise Old Owl
Grade: A

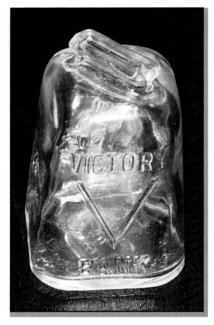

No.: AG-100
Name: Victory Bank, Save Dimes for Defense
Height: 3⅜"
Slot: raised diagonal slot
Info: clear glass; Front — Victory Bank; Back — Save Dimes for Defense Bonds
Grade: Rare

No.: AG-101
Name: Wise Old Owl, Libbey
Height: 6¼"
Slot: raised
Info: brown glass; Libbey of Canada on bottom in small letters between Wise Old Owl
Grade: A

No.: AG-102
Name: Big Eyed Owl
Height: 6½"
Slot: molded in back of head
Info: dark amber glass, also clear glass; ⅜" hole in bottom center; Label — Cascade England
Grade: D

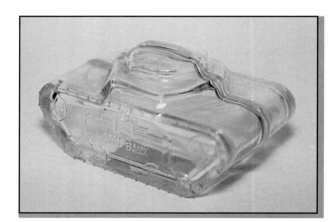

No.: AG-103
Name: Tank
Height: 2¼"
Slot: molded-in seam
Info: clear glass, split-apart type; Coin Bank on both sides; Label — green paper To Break Instructions
Grade: E

See page 7 for price ranges.

No.: AG-104
Name: Teddy Bear
Height: 6"
Slot: raised
Info: clear glass; Anchor Hocking
Grade: A

No.:   AG-105
Name: Arched Back Pig
Height: 5¾"
Slot: cut-in top
Info: dark smoke glass; Cascade, England
Grade: D

No.:   AG-106
Name: Mickey Mouse Club
Height: 6¾"
Slot: raised
Info: dark smoke glass; Back —
Mickey Mouse Club; Bottom — Walt
Disney Productions
Grade: B

No.:   AG-107
Name: Mickey Mouse Club
Height: 6¾"
Slot: raised
Info: smoke frosted glass; Back
— Mickey Mouse Club; Bottom —
Walt Disney Productions
Grade: B

No.:   AG-108
Name: Mickey Mouse Club
Height: 6¾"
Slot: raised
Info: light green glass; Back —
Mickey Mouse Club; Bottom — Walt
Disney Productions
Grade: C

No.:   AG-109
Name: Mickey Mouse Club
Height: 6⅞"
Slot: raised
Info: blue glass, Taiwanese repro-
duction; Back — Mickey Mouse Club;
Bottom — Walt Disney Productions
Grade: A

RATING/GRADING	
A	To $15.00
B	$15.00 – 35.00
C	$35.00 – 75.00
D	$75.00 – 150.00
E	$150.00 – 300.00
F	$300.00 – 600.00
Rare	$600.00 – 1,000.00
Very Rare	negotiable

No.: AG-110
NAME: Indian Chief
HEIGHT: 6"
SLOT: raised
INFO: dark amber, 1983; Bottom — Thank You, FIG in a bottle shape, clear, 1981
GRADE: D, clear glass: F

No.: AG-111
NAME: Glass Float with String Holder
HEIGHT: 3⅛"
SLOT: raised
INFO: light green glass, Jute string holder
GRADE: C

No.: AG-112
NAME: Pig with Tulips
HEIGHT: 3⅝"
SLOT: raised round slot
INFO: clear glass with tulip pattern; Taiwan, not marked
GRADE: D

No.: AG-113
NAME: Hello Kitty
HEIGHT: 6⅞"
SLOT: raised round slot
INFO: clear frosted, clear bluish, pink; Paper Tag — 1998 Sanrio Co. Ltd.
GRADE: D

No.:   AG-114
NAME: Sitting Lion
HEIGHT: 6¾"
SLOT: raised round slot
INFO: dark blue glass
GRADE: D

No.:   AG-115
NAME: Large Glass Float
HEIGHT: 5⁷⁄₁₆"
SLOT: raised round slot
INFO: green glass sitting in clear coaster, Jute string holder; height is float alone
GRADE: D

No.:   AG-116
NAME: Vertical Fish
HEIGHT: 6"
SLOT: raised round slot
INFO: clear glass
GRADE: D

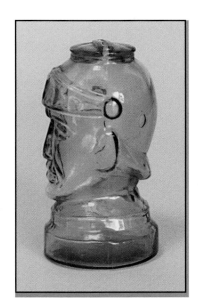

No.:   AG-117
NAME: Roman Soldier Bust
HEIGHT: 6³⁄₁₆"
SLOT: raised round slot
INFO: light green glass
GRADE: D

ALL GLASS BANKS – MOLDED BANKS

No.: AG-118
Name: Owl
Height: 4⅞"
Slot: raised round slot
Info: medium green glass
Grade: D

No.: AG-119
Name: Pig with Bow in Hair
Height: 6"
Slot: raised round slot
Info: purple, green
Grade: D

No.: AG-120
Name: San Francisco Trolley
Height: 4¾"
Slot: raised round slot
Info: blue, amethyst
Grade: D

No.: AG-121
Name: Woman Bust
Height: 7⅛"
Slot: raised round slot
Info: clear, green
Grade: D

No.: AG-122
Name: Automobile
Height: 4⅝"
Slot: raised round slot
Info: clear glass
Grade: D

No.: AG-123
Name: Boy in Boat
Height: 6⅝"
Slot: raised round slot
Info: purple, blue
Grade: D

RATING/GRADING	
A	To $15.00
B	$15.00 – 35.00
C	$35.00 – 75.00
D	$75.00 – 150.00
E	$150.00 – 300.00
F	$300.00 – 600.00
Rare	$600.00 – 1,000.00
Very Rare	negotiable

No.: AG-124
Name: Sitting Dog
Height: 6"
Slot: raised round slot
Info: green glass
Grade: D

Flask Banks

NO.: FL-1
NAME: Large Eagle
HEIGHT: 6"
SLOT: raised
INFO: carnival glass
GRADE: B

NO.: FL-2
NAME: Small Eagle
HEIGHT: 4⁷⁄₁₆"
SLOT: raised
INFO: carnival glass
GRADE: B

NO.: FL-3
NAME: Small Eagle, Coca-Cola
HEIGHT: 4³⁄₈"
SLOT: raised
INFO: blue glass with screened writing in white; Taiwan
GRADE: B

NO.: FL-4
NAME: Small Eagle, Pepsi Cola
HEIGHT: 4³⁄₈"
SLOT: raised
INFO: milk glass with screened writing in red; Taiwan
GRADE: B

NO.: FL-5
NAME: Small Eagle, large, Coca-Cola
HEIGHT: 4⅜"
SLOT: raised
INFO: milk glass with screened writing in gold;
Taiwan; Coca-Cola in large letters
GRADE: B

NO.: FL-6
NAME: Small Eagle, Coca-Cola
HEIGHT: 4⅜"
SLOT: raised
INFO: milk glass with screened writing in red;
Taiwan; Coca-Cola in small letters
GRADE: B

NO.: FL-7
NAME: Buffalo Nickel
HEIGHT: 6⅝"
SLOT: raised
INFO: clear glass, Anchor Hocking
GRADE: A

NO.: FL-8
NAME: Small Eagle
HEIGHT: 4⅜"
SLOT: raised
INFO: rose, green, blue; Taiwan
GRADE: A

NO.: FL-9
NAME: Mickey & Minnie
HEIGHT: 6⅝"
SLOT: raised
INFO: clear glass; Anchor Hocking; Bottom — The Walt Disney Co.
GRADE: A

NO.: FL-10
NAME: Thomas Mellon
HEIGHT: 6⅝"
SLOT: raised
INFO: clear glass
GRADE: D

NO.: FL-11
NAME: Small Eagle
HEIGHT: 4⁵⁄₁₆"
SLOT: raised
INFO: cobalt blue glass with screened image of Hopalong Cassidy
GRADE: D

NO.: FL-12
NAME: Eleven Years of Excellence
HEIGHT: 6⅝"
SLOT: raised
INFO: clear glass with image etched
GRADE: D

No.: FL-13
NAME: Small Eagle, Shirley Temple
HEIGHT: 4⁵⁄₁₆"
SLOT: raised
INFO: milk glass with image screened in blue; Taiwan
GRADE: D

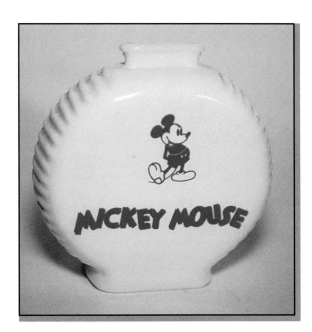

No.: FL-14
NAME: Small Eagle, Mickey Mouse
HEIGHT: 4⁵⁄₁₆"
SLOT: raised
INFO: milk glass with image screened in red
GRADE: D

RATING/GRADING	
A	To $15.00
B	$15.00 – 35.00
C	$35.00 – 75.00
D	$75.00 – 150.00
E	$150.00 – 300.00
F	$300.00 – 600.00
Rare	$600.00 – 1,000.00
Very Rare	negotiable

No.: FL-15
NAME: Cedarburg, 1885 – 1985
HEIGHT: 6⁵⁄₈"
SLOT: raised
INFO: clear glass with image screened in dark green
GRADE: D

Bottle Necks with Side Slot Flasks

NO.: FLB-1
NAME: The Jersey Devil
HEIGHT: 7¾"
SLOT: molded in side
INFO: purple glass; Clevenger Bros., Clayton, N.J.
GRADE: B

NO.: FLB-2
NAME: George Washington 1st National State Bank
HEIGHT: 7¾"
SLOT: molded in side
INFO: dark green glass; Clevenger Bros., Clayton, N.J.
GRADE: C

NO.: FLB-3
NAME: Brockton Savings, 100th Anniversary
HEIGHT: 7¾"
SLOT: molded in side
INFO: light blue glass; Clevenger Bros., Clayton, N.J.
GRADE: C

NO.: FLB-4
NAME: World's Fair 1982, Knoxville, Tennessee
HEIGHT: 7¾"
SLOT: molded in side
INFO: light green, light amber; Dart Ad. Inc., Henderson, N.E.
GRADE: B

NO.: FLB-5
NAME: Anchor Hocking Container, Plant #6, Gene Gavin
HEIGHT: 7¾"
SLOT: molded in side
INFO: medium dark blue glass; Clevenger Bros., Clayton, N.J.
GRADE: B

NO.: FLB-6
NAME: Oklahoma 75th Diamond Jubilee, 1982
HEIGHT: 7¾"
SLOT: molded in side
INFO: light green glass; Dart Ad. Inc., Henderson, N.E.
GRADE: B

NO.: FLB-7
NAME: Old Barney Lighthouse, Barnegat Light
HEIGHT: 7¾"
SLOT: molded in side
INFO: cobalt blue glass; Clevenger Bros., Clayton, N.J.
GRADE: B

NO.: FLB-8
NAME: Hagerstown Trust Co.
HEIGHT: 7¾"
SLOT: molded in side
INFO: medium green glass; Clevenger Bros., Clayton, N.J.
GRADE: B

NO.: FLB-9
NAME: Valley Bank and Trust
HEIGHT: 7¾"
SLOT: molded in side
INFO: medium green glass; Clevenger Bros., Clayton, N.J.
GRADE: B

NO.: FLB-10
NAME: The Ephrata National Bank, 100 Years, 1881 – 1981
HEIGHT: 7¾"
SLOT: molded in side
INFO: light blue glass; Clevenger Bros., Clayton, N.J.
GRADE: B

NO.: FLB-11
NAME: Anchor Hocking 1980, Merry Christmas and Happy New Year
HEIGHT: 7¾"
SLOT: molded in side
INFO: medium blue glass; Clevenger Bros., Clayton, N.J.
GRADE: C

NO.: FLB-12
NAME: City of Taneytown, Maryland, 100th Anniversary, 1884 – 1984
HEIGHT: 7¾"
SLOT: molded in side
INFO: light green glass; Clevenger Bros., Clayton, N.J.
GRADE: B

No.:   FLB-13
NAME: Ben Franklin Kite Experiment, June 1752
HEIGHT: 7¾"
SLOT: molded in side
INFO: purple glass; Clevenger Bros., Clayton, N.J.
GRADE: B

No.:   FLB-14
NAME: Hanover Numismatic Society 20th Anniv.,
          1963 –1993
HEIGHT: 7¾"
SLOT: molded in side
INFO: dark blue glass; Clevenger Bros., Clayton, N.J.
GRADE: B

See page 7 for price ranges.

No.:   FLB-15
NAME: Elvis Presley January 8, 1935, 1983 EPE Inc.
HEIGHT: 7¾"
SLOT: molded in style
INFO: dark blue glass; Graceland, Memphis, Aug
16, 1977; Clevenger Bros., Clayton, N.J.
GRADE: D

No.:   FLB-16
NAME: Rena Ware, Catch the Rena Ware Spirit
HEIGHT: 7¾"
SLOT: molded in side
INFO: light blue glass; Clevenger Bros., Clayton, N.J.
GRADE: C

No.: FLB-17
Name: George Washington 250th Birthday Anniversary, 1732 – 1982
Height: 7¾"
Slot: molded in side
Info: light blue glass; Supreme Council Northern Masonic Jurisdiction; Clevenger Bros., Clayton, N.J.
Grade: B

No.: FLB-18
Name: Joseph C. Cordery, Happy Retirement, Jan. 31, 1970 – May 31, 1997
Height: 7¾"
Slot: molded in side
Info: cobalt blue glass; GMP Local 21, Anchor Glass; Clevenger Bros., Clayton, N.J.
Grade: B

No.: FLB-19
Name: Grit Publishing Co., Williamsport, Pa., 1882 – 1982
Height: 7⁹⁄₁₆"
Slot: molded in side
Info: light green glass; Clevenger Bros., Clayton, N.J.
Grade: C

No.: FLB-20
Name: Old Court House 1750, Shippensburg, Pa.
Height: 7¾"
Slot: molded in glass
Info: blue green glass; Valley Bank & Trust Founded 1807; Clevenger Bros., Clayton, N.J.
Grade: B

No.: FLB-21
Name: Delaware Trust Co.
Height: 7¾"
Slot: molded in glass
Info: medium blue glass; large griffin on one
side; Clevenger Bros., Clayton, N.J.
Grade: B

No.: FLB-22
Name: Colonial Federal Savings & Loan, Quincy
Holbrook, Weymouth, Wareham
Height: 7¾"
Slot: molded in side
Info: light green glass; 1706 Ben Franklin 1790;
Clevenger Bros., Clayton, N.J.
Grade: B

See page 7 for price ranges.

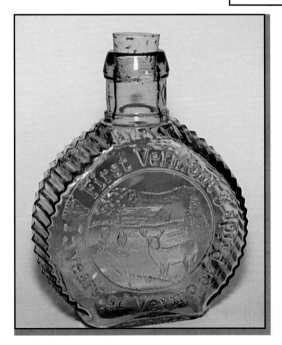

No.: FLB-23
Name: First Vermont, 75 Years of Vermont Pride, 1906 – 1981
Height: 7¾"
Slot: molded in side
Info: aqua colored glass; Clevenger Bros., Clayton, N.J.
Grade: B

No.: FLB-24
Name: Orange County Trust Company, Since 1892
Height: 7¾"
Slot: molded in style
Info: aqua colored glass; 1706 Ben Franklin
1790; Clevenger Bros., Clayton, N.J.
Grade: B

Combination Glass Banks

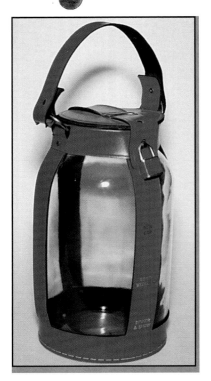

No.: CG-1
NAME: Lantern Design Jar
HEIGHT: 8¾"
SLOT: formed brass slot in top
INFO: clear glass and red leather; money levels — Mink, New Car, Long Weekend, Dinner & Show; Griffin USA
GRADE: B

No.: CG-2
NAME: Lantern Design Jar
HEIGHT: 8¾"
SLOT: formed brass slot in top
INFO: clear glass and black leather; money levels — Mink, New Car, Long Weekend, Dinner & Show; Griffin USA
GRADE: A

No.: CG-3
NAME: Lantern Design Jar
HEIGHT: 7⅛"
SLOT: formed brass slot in top
INFO: clear glass and black leather; money levels — Europe, Jaguar, Long Weekend, Dinner & Show; Major Metal Fabricators
GRADE: B

No.: CG-5
NAME: Lock Top Square Jar
HEIGHT: 4⅝"
SLOT: formed brass slot in top
INFO: clear glass and leather
GRADE: C

RATING/GRADING	
A	To $15.00
B	$15.00 – 35.00
C	$35.00 – 75.00
D	$75.00 – 150.00
E	$150.00 – 300.00
F	$300.00 – 600.00
Rare	$600.00 – 1,000.00
Very Rare	negotiable

No.: CG-4
NAME: Double Your Money Magnifying Jar
HEIGHT: 5"
SLOT: formed brass in side lid
INFO: clear glass and black leather; magnifying glass in lid; real hide, Made in England
GRADE: C

NO.: CG-6
NAME: Algonquin Park Canada Jar
HEIGHT: 3½"
SLOT: punched in top
INFO: clear glass and leather; Savings and Loan, Watch the Money Grow; Canada
GRADE: B

NO.: CG-7
NAME: Savings Bank Niagara Falls Jar
HEIGHT: 3⁹⁄₁₆"
SLOT: punched in top
INFO: clear glass and leather; Watch the Money, Climb the Ladder; NFC Canada
GRADE: B

NO.: CG-8
NAME: Savings Bank Rainbow Bridge Canada Jar
HEIGHT: 3⅝"
SLOT: punched in top
INFO: clear glass; leather covered lid only; Canada
GRADE: B

NO.: CG-9
NAME: Small Pig Milk Bottle
HEIGHT: 4"
SLOT: formed brass slot in nose
INFO: clear glass and leather, half pint; brass rivet eyes and feet
GRADE: C

NO.: CG-10
NAME: Lantern Globe, Pat. Aug 2, 1898
HEIGHT: 3⅝"
SLOT: punched in top
INFO: aluminum and clear glass; Wm. H. Dietz
GRADE: D

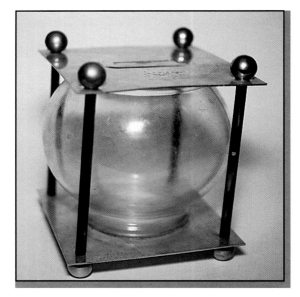

No.: CG-11
Name: Boxed Globe
Height: 5⅜"
Slot: punched in top
Info: aluminum top and bottom, steel posts and balls; Wm. H. Dietz, 115 Dearborn St, Chicago, Pat. Aug 2, 1898
Grade: C

No.: CG-12
Name: Lantern Globe
Height: 4"
Slot: formed in plastic top
Info: clear glass and plastic; Wm. H. Dietz, Chicago
Grade: D

No.: CG-13
Name: Box
Height: 6⅛"
Slot: punched in top
Info: clear glass and steel; Wm. H. Dietz, Chicago, Ilinois, Pat. Nov. 14, 1899; key locked front
Grade: C

No.: CG-14
Name: Crystal Lattice Top
Height: 4"
Slot: molded in top
Info: clear glass vertical ribs and cast iron; Arcade Mfg.
Grade: D

No.: CG-15
Name: Crystal Solid Top
Height: 3¾"
Slot: molded in top
Info: clear glass vertical ribs and cast iron; Arcade Mfg.
Grade: E

No.: CG-16
NAME: Large Tent
HEIGHT: 5¼"
SLOT: molded in top
INFO: plain clear glass and cast iron; painted silver top and bottom
GRADE: E

No.: CG-17
NAME: Small Tent
HEIGHT: 4¾"
SLOT: molded in top
INFO: plain clear glass and cast iron; painted gold top and bottom
GRADE: E

No.: CG-18
NAME: Clock Shaped Collection Bank
HEIGHT: 7"
SLOT: punched in top
INFO: clear glass and sheet steel; has four wooden feet; key locked bottom trap
GRADE: C

RATING/GRADING	
A	To $15.00
B	$15.00 – 35.00
C	$35.00 – 75.00
D	$75.00 – 150.00
E	$150.00 – 300.00
F	$300.00 – 600.00
Rare	$600.00 – 1,000.00
Very Rare	negotiable

No.: CG-19
NAME: Cylinder
HEIGHT: 5¾"
SLOT: punched bottom slot
INFO: clear glass and copper-plated steel; 1st National Bank of Leechburg, Pa.; red felt on inside bottom; small top, square ring handle
GRADE: B

No.: CG-20
NAME: Cylinder
HEIGHT: 5¾"
SLOT: punched bottom slot
INFO: clear glass and steel; large top, round ring holder
GRADE: B

No.: CG-21
NAME: Cylinder Bank
HEIGHT: 5¾"
SLOT: punched bottom slot
INFO: clear glass and steel; large top, square Pat. Pend ring holder
GRADE: B

No.: CG-22
NAME: Hour Glass
HEIGHT: 9¼"
SLOT: punched in brass top
INFO: amber glass; wood, tin, rubber, brass; Bottom — Tin Locking Coin Trap
GRADE: C

No.: CG-23
NAME: Junior J.T.'s Bubble Gum Bank Clown
HEIGHT: 6¾"
SLOT: punched in side
INFO: clear glass and steel, red machine; United Metal Products, Boston, Mass.
GRADE: D

No.: CG-24
NAME: Postal Savings
HEIGHT: 4¾"
SLOT: punched under lid flap
INFO: clear glass and steel; Postal Savings Bank, U.S. Mail; nickel plated
GRADE: C

No.: CG-25
NAME: Horse Head in Horseshoe
HEIGHT: 3¼"
SLOT: molded in end
INFO: clear glass and aluminum
GRADE: D

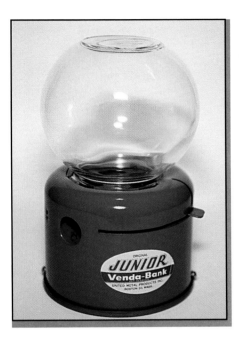

NO.: CG-26
NAME: Junior Venda-Bank Bubble Gum Machine
HEIGHT: 6¾"
SLOT: punched in side
INFO: clear glass and steel, green machine; United Metal Products, Boston, Mass.
GRADE: C

NO.: CG-27
NAME: Junior Bubble Ball Gum Bank
HEIGHT: 6⅜"
SLOT: punched in side
INFO: clear glass and steel, smaller blue machine; United Metal Products, Boston, Mass.
GRADE: D

NO.: CG-28
NAME: Carousel Gum Ball Machine
HEIGHT: 14½"
SLOT: molded in front
INFO: clear glass and diecast zinc, red machine; Carousel Industries, Ill.; Large No. 84
GRADE: B

NO.: CG-29
NAME: Carousel Gum Ball Machine
HEIGHT: 11¼"
SLOT: molded in front
INFO: clear glass and diecast zinc, red machine; Carousel Industries, Ill.; Medium No. 89-B
GRADE: B

NO.: CG-30
NAME: Small Carousel Gum Ball Machine
HEIGHT: 8½"
SLOT: molded in front
INFO: clear glass, red machine; Carousel Industries, Ill.
GRADE: B

153

No.: CG-31
NAME: Lead Crystal Baby Shoe
HEIGHT: 2¾"
SLOT: molded in top
INFO: clear patterned glass and steel; Crystal Legends by Godinger, 24% Lead Crystal, West Germany; steel key locked bottom
GRADE: D

No.: CG-32
NAME: Buck Bank
HEIGHT: 8"
SLOT: large dollar slot in top
INFO: clear etched glass and wood, $100 Bill, Private Reserve, Buck Bank; slot has wooden push stick
GRADE: C

No.: CG-33
NAME: Large Souvenir Barrel
HEIGHT: 10½"
SLOT: punched in wood top
INFO: Treasure Barrel, amber glass, wood, brass
GRADE: C

No.: CG-34
NAME: Medium Souvenir Barrel
HEIGHT: 7⅛"
SLOT: punched in wood top
INFO: Maine, amber glass, wood, brass
GRADE: B

RATING/GRADING	
A	To $15.00
B	$15.00 – 35.00
C	$35.00 – 75.00
D	$75.00 – 150.00
E	$150.00 – 300.00
F	$300.00 – 600.00
Rare	$600.00 – 1,000.00
Very Rare	negotiable

No.: CG-35
NAME: Small Souvenir Barrel
HEIGHT: 5½"
SLOT: punched in wood top
INFO: Boot Hill, Dodge City, Kansas, amber glass, wood, brass
GRADE: B

No.: CG-36
NAME: Small Souvenir Barrel
HEIGHT: 5½"
SLOT: punched in wood top
INFO: Knoxville, Tennessee, The 1982 World's Fair, amber glass, wood, brass
GRADE: B

No.: CG-37
NAME: Small Souvenir Barrel
HEIGHT: 5½"
SLOT: punched in wood top
INFO: Beer, reasons to drink beer, amber glass, wood, brass
GRADE: B

No.: CG-38
NAME: Goebel Baby Pig
HEIGHT: 4¾"
SLOT: raised slot
INFO: clear crystal glass with flower designs; Kristah-glas; Go; metal key lock bottom trap
GRADE: D

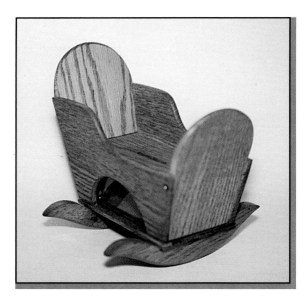

No.: CG-39
NAME: Teddy Bear Holding Small Teddy Bear Baby
HEIGHT: 4⅞"
SLOT: cut in top
INFO: clear crystal glass with frosted areas; Label — Crystal Legends by Godinger, 24% Lead Crystal, Made in West Germany
GRADE: D

No.: CG-40
NAME: The Thornville Banking Co. Dome
HEIGHT: 4¹⁄₁₆"
SLOT: side metal-edged slot
INFO: clear glass with cut glass flower design on top; screened gold lettering and trim; Bottom — Sweet-Forschile, New Orleans, Pat. Applied For
GRADE: E

No.: CG-41
NAME: Cradle
HEIGHT: 7⅝"
SLOT: cut in top
INFO: oak clear glass sides; end unscrews to retrieve coins
GRADE: D

No.: CG-42
NAME: Fort Knox Safe
HEIGHT: 7¾"
SLOT: punched in top
INFO: glass jar bank screws to top of safe under slot; Top — Times-Democrat, Top 25% Carrier Award; steel, plastic dial
GRADE: E

NO.: CG-43
NAME: Small Souvenir Barrel
HEIGHT: 5½"
SLOT: punched in wood
INFO: Pennsylvania Dutch Country, amber glass, wood, brass
GRADE: B

NO.: CG-44
NAME: Small Souvenir Barrel
HEIGHT: 5½"
SLOT: punched in wood
INFO: Atlantic City, gambling, amber glass, wood, brass
GRADE: B

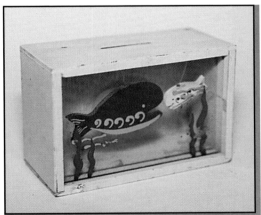

NO.: CG-45
NAME: Large Pillsbury Doughboy, 25th Anniversary Gum Ball Machine
HEIGHT: 19"
SLOT: molded in front
INFO: glass Doughboy with painted eyes, diecast zinc, blue machine, cloth hat and white scarf; Happy 25th Birthday on Gum Balls; Carousel Industries, Taiwan
GRADE: F

NO.: CG-46
NAME: Fish Tank
HEIGHT: 3⅛"
SLOT: cut in top
INFO: fish hang on strings between two pieces of glass; plastic coin trap in back, wood with glass front
GRADE: C

NO.: CG-47
NAME: Little Sprout Green Jelly Bean Machine
HEIGHT: 12½"
SLOT: molded in front
INFO: clear glass Little Sprout with painted eyes, diecast zinc, green machine, green plastic hat; Carousel, Taiwan
GRADE: D

RATING/GRADING	
A	To $15.00
B	$15.00 – 35.00
C	$35.00 – 75.00
D	$75.00 – 150.00
E	$150.00 – 300.00
F	$300.00 – 600.00
Rare	$600.00 – 1,000.00
Very Rare	negotiable

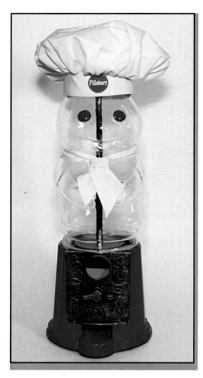

No.:   CG-48
NAME: Small Pillsbury Doughboy
       White Jelly Bean Machine
HEIGHT: 13"
SLOT: molded in front
INFO: clear glass Doughboy with
painted eyes, diecast zinc, blue
machine, cloth hat and white scarf;
Carousel, Taiwan
GRADE: D

No.:   CG-49
NAME: White Lantern Globe
HEIGHT: 5½"
SLOT: punched in top
INFO: clear glass lantern globe with
white painted steel top and bottom; red felt
inside bottom; SB130
GRADE: D

No.:   CG-50
NAME: Cape Cod Mass Log Slice Savings
       Bank
HEIGHT: 5"
SLOT: punched in tin back
INFO: hand-painted scene on tin back;
painted scene on flat front glass; Savings
Bank on domed glass front
GRADE: C

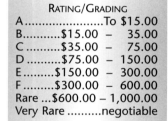

RATING/GRADING	
A	To $15.00
B	$15.00 – 35.00
C	$35.00 – 75.00
D	$75.00 – 150.00
E	$150.00 – 300.00
F	$300.00 – 600.00
Rare	$600.00 – 1,000.00
Very Rare	negotiable

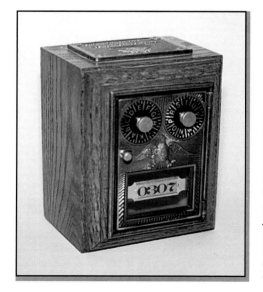

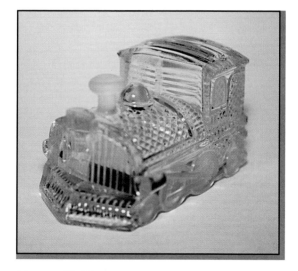

No.:   CG-51
NAME: Post Office Box
HEIGHT: 6½"
SLOT: molded in top
INFO: brass lock box door
and oak wood, cast brass
plate on top; Bottom Label —
Jolly Good Industries Inc.,
2001 Corporate Dr., Boynton
Beach, FL.; two dials with
eagle
GRADE: C

No.:   CG-52
NAME: Locomotive
HEIGHT: 3"
SLOT: molded in top
INFO: clear crystal glass with etched areas, bot-
tom key lock coin trap; Label — Crystal Legends by
Godinger, 24% Lead Crystal, Made in West Ger-
many
GRADE: D

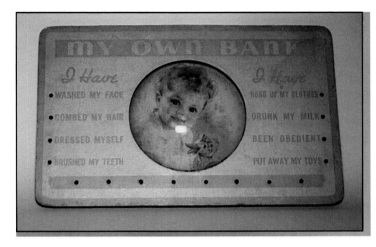

No.: CG-53
NAME: Baby Block
HEIGHT: 3"
SLOT: molded in top
INFO: clear crystal glass with etched area, bottom key lock coin trap; Label — Crystal Legends by Godinger, 24% Lead Crystal, Made in West Germany
GRADE: D

No.: CG-54
NAME: My Own Bank, Baby with Duck Toy
HEIGHT: 7" x 11"
SLOT: formed in top
INFO: light blue printing on white; coins drop in top to glass dome; peg holes for marking jobs complete; swing out leg in back for standing
GRADE: D

No.: CG-55
NAME: Small Souvenir Barrel
HEIGHT: 5½"
SLOT: punched in wood top
INFO: Niagara Falls Canada, Bridal Veil Falls, blue plastic label bonded to glass
GRADE: B

No.: CG-56
NAME: Buddy Bank Mechanical
HEIGHT: 4¼"
SLOT: punched in lid
INFO: tin and glass; place coin in hand over slot, shake other hand, coin is deposited; Mar Toys, Made in USA
GRADE: E

No.: CG-57
NAME: Remember Bank
HEIGHT: 7" x 11"
SLOT: formed in top
INFO: red printing on white; coins drop in top to glass dome; peg holes for marking items to buy at the store; swing out leg in back for standing; for kitchen use, picture flowers
GRADE: D

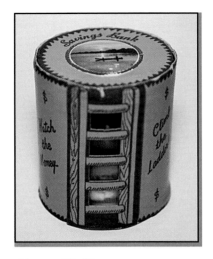

No.: CG-58
NAME: Savings Canoe Scene
HEIGHT: 3⅝"
SLOT: punched in top
INFO: Medicine Hat, Canada, 1867 – 1967; Watch the Money, Climb the Ladder; covered glass jar
GRADE: B

No.: CG-59
NAME: Duck Gum Ball Machine
HEIGHT: 8¾"
SLOT: molded in neck
INFO: clear glass globe with painted multicolor duck machine and diecast zinc; also found color variation and one brass plated; Carousel Industries Inc., Des Plaines, Ill., Taiwan
GRADE: E

No.: CG-60
NAME: Coach Lamp
HEIGHT: 7⅞"
SLOT: punched in top
INFO: black or red with clear glass and tin; Box — Thayer Savings Bank, Blackwood, N.J.; red — No. 7001, black — No. 7002, Made In Hong Kong
GRADE: C

RATING/GRADING	
A	To $15.00
B	$15.00 – 35.00
C	$35.00 – 75.00
D	$75.00 – 150.00
E	$150.00 – 300.00
F	$300.00 – 600.00
Rare	$600.00 – 1,000.00
Very Rare	negotiable

NO.: CG-61
NAME: Eagle Magnifying
HEIGHT: 4⅜"
SLOT: punched in side
INFO: magnifying glass lid set in brass colored lid and bank, diecast zinc eagle; cardboard and brass bottom trap
GRADE: D

NO.: CG-62
NAME: American Institute of Child Life
        After School Club Safe
HEIGHT: 3½"
SLOT: two punched in top
INFO: clear glass with tin top and inside divider, padlock bottom; Sides — Parents Slotted Compartment, Young Folks Slotted Compartment, Pat. Applied For
GRADE: E

NO.: CG-63
NAME: Batman & Robin Gum Ball
        Machine
HEIGHT: 16"
SLOT: molded in front
INFO: should have Batman and Robin figures on top
GRADE: C

NO.: CG-64
NAME: Locomotive Engine No. 9 Gum Ball Machine
HEIGHT: 9¼"
SLOT: molded in back
INFO: clear glass globe with red diecast zinc machine; Also found in blue; Taiwan S C
GRADE: E

No.: CG-66
NAME: His and Hers Lantern Design Twin Jars
HEIGHT: 7½"
SLOT: formed brass slots in top
INFO: clear glass square jars with brown and ivory leather, one padlock; also found in red and black
GRADE: C

No.: CG-65
NAME: Pig 1 Cent
HEIGHT: 7½"
SLOT: cut in top
INFO: wooden pig with rope tail, clear glass screened in red and white; deposits points to coin slot; loans points to cork trap
GRADE: C

No.: CG-67
NAME: Hers and Hers Lantern Design Twin Jars
HEIGHT: 6¾"
SLOT: formed brass slots in top
INFO: clear oval shaped glass jars with horizontal ribbed edges; black and red leather, two padlocks; Shields Style No. 1281, Japan
GRADE: D

No.: CG-68
NAME: Pay Phone Booth
HEIGHT: 8"
SLOT: punched in top
INFO: clear glass in rubbed black finish tin bank; arrow on roof points to coin slot; round metal bottom trap
GRADE: C

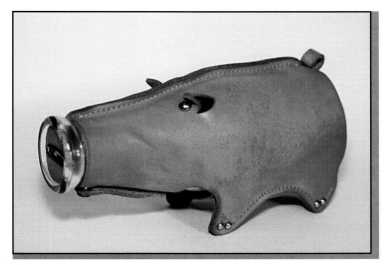

No.: CG-69
NAME: Horizontal Vault
HEIGHT: 3⅜"
SLOT: formed in tower top
INFO: mechanical, put coin in tower box on top, press down on box, coin is deposited; Stavanger O G, Rogalands Bank A.S., Bosse Nr. 3008, key lock top trap; nickel-plated brass and glass
GRADE: E

No.: CG-70
NAME: Large Pig Milk Bottle
HEIGHT: 4⅞"
SLOT: formed brass slot in nose
INFO: clear glass quart bottle covered in leather; brass rivet eyes and feet
GRADE: D

No.: CG-72
NAME: Save for Victory, Uncle Sam
HEIGHT: 7" x 11"
SLOT: formed in top
INFO: red, white, and blue on light blue; coins drop in top slot to glass dome area; swing out leg in back for standing; cardboard
GRADE: E

No.: CG-71
NAME: Post Office Box Letter Drop
HEIGHT: 9"
SLOT: cut in back
INFO: made from post office lock box, brass door and pine wood, single dial
GRADE: C

See page 7 for price ranges.

No.: CG-73
NAME: Frog Lantern
HEIGHT: 6⅛"
SLOT: open mouth
INFO: light amber glass globe in red, painted tin frog; bottom trap; bail handle
GRADE: D

No.: CG-74
NAME: School House
HEIGHT: 9⅜"
SLOT: cut in back
INFO: made from post office lock box with chair, dunce hat, bell, flag; souvenir of Oakhurst, CA, Original P.O. Door 1959 – 1994, Howdy's, P.O. Box 1995, Oakhurst, CA, 93644; wood, brass, and glass
GRADE: C

No.: CG-75
NAME: Planters Peanut Machine
HEIGHT: 12¾"
SLOT: cut in front
INFO: clear glass globe, wooden machine with paper label; Knock on Wood Corp., San Dimas, CA, Made in USA
GRADE: B

No.: CG-76
NAME: Large P.O. Box Door
HEIGHT: 7¾"
SLOT: cut in back
INFO: made from post office lock box; Souvenir of Oakhurst, CA, Original P.O. Door 1959 – 1994, Howdy's, P.O. Box 1995, Oakhurst, CA 93644; wood, brass, and glass
GRADE: C

No.: CG-77
NAME: Molson Golden Imported
HEIGHT: 10¼"
SLOT: cut in top
INFO: paper covered wood with masonite; image screened on inside of glass; Martlet Importing Co. Inc., Great Neck, N.Y.
GRADE: C

No.: CG-78
NAME: Medium Souvenir Barrel
HEIGHT: 7⅛"
SLOT: punched in wood top
INFO: South of the Border, South Carolina, amber glass, brass, and wood
GRADE: B

No.: CG-79
NAME: Save for Victory, MacArthur Bank
HEIGHT: 7" x 11"
SLOT: formed in top
INFO: red, white, and blue on light blue; coins drop in top slot to glass dome area; swing out leg in back for standing; cardboard and glass
GRADE: D

No.: CG-80
NAME: Crystal Mushroom
HEIGHT: 4⅛"
SLOT: cut in top
INFO: clear glass with frosted spots and base; Goebel-Kristahglas, West Germany; metal key lock trap bottom
GRADE: D

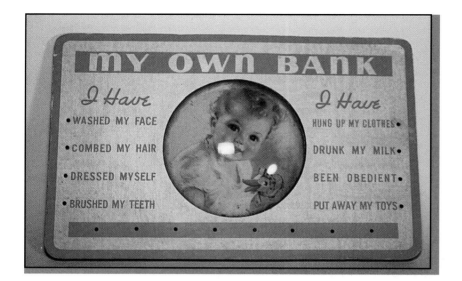

NO.: CG-81
NAME: My Own Bank, Baby with Toy Duck
HEIGHT: 7" x 11"
SLOT: formed in top
INFO: red printed on white; coins drop in top to glass dome; peg holes for marking jobs complete; swing out leg in back for standing; cardboard and glass
GRADE: D

NO.: CG-82
NAME: Baby Bottle
HEIGHT: 6¼"
SLOT: cut in top
INFO: clear pressed glass with $ molded in front; Top — nickel-plated brass
GRADE: D

RATING/GRADING	
A.......................To	$15.00
B...........$15.00 –	35.00
C.........$35.00 –	75.00
D.........$75.00 –	150.00
E.........$150.00 –	300.00
F.........$300.00 –	600.00
Rare ...$600.00 –	1,000.00
Very Rare ....negotiable	

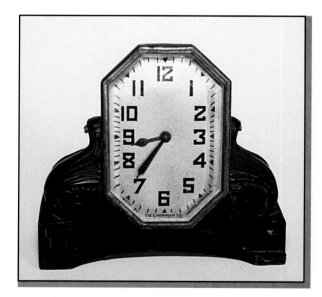

NO.: CG-83
NAME: Hidden Slot Clock
HEIGHT: 4¼"
SLOT: base behind clock
INFO: There are many clock banks with glass fronts on the clock face. This book does not include all of these clocks. This one was chosen as an unusual example. The Ingram Co., Bristol, Conn.
GRADE: D

NO.: CG-84
NAME: Glass Front Cross, By This Sign Conquer
HEIGHT: 8⅞"
SLOT: molded in top
INFO: cast iron bank with glass front, sheet brass trap in base; A David C. Cook Product Pat
GRADE: F

NO.: CG-85
NAME: The Banker Lantern Design Jar
HEIGHT: 8⅞"
SLOT: formed brass slot in top
INFO: clear glass round jar with black plastic faux leather; came originally with candy; Houston Foods Inc., Chicago, Ill.
GRADE: C

NO.: CG-86
NAME: Gum Ball Machine
HEIGHT: 9"
SLOT: molded in front
INFO: clear glass globe, light blue diecast zinc machine; Taiwan 1985; seals with ball on front
GRADE: B

RATING/GRADING	
A	To $15.00
B	$15.00 – 35.00
C	$35.00 – 75.00
D	$75.00 – 150.00
E	$150.00 – 300.00
F	$300.00 – 600.00
Rare	$600.00 – 1,000.00
Very Rare	negotiable

NO.: CG-87
NAME: David C. Cook Globe
HEIGHT: 7⅞"
SLOT: punched in top
INFO: clear glass globe with nickel-plated brass top and bottom; bottom trap with padlock; David C. Cook, Publishing Co., Elgin, Ill.
GRADE: E

NO.: CG-88
NAME: Gum Ball Machine
HEIGHT: 9"
SLOT: molded in front
INFO: clear glass globe, red diecast zinc machine; Carousel Industries, Taiwan 1985; children hand in hand and flowers on front
GRADE: B

NO.:   CG-89
NAME: Small Souvenir Barrel
HEIGHT: 5½"
SLOT: punched in wood top
INFO: Grant's Farm, Grant's Cabin; amber glass, wood, and brass
GRADE: B

NO.:   CG-90
NAME: Small Souvenir Barrel
HEIGHT: 5½"
SLOT: punched in wood top
INFO: Fascination Island, Memory Okinawa; wood, glass, and brass
GRADE: B

NO.:   CG-91
NAME: Goebel Money Bags
HEIGHT: 5⁷⁄₁₆"
SLOT: cut in top
INFO: clear crystal glass with frosted areas; Goebel-Kristahglas, West Germany
GRADE: D

NO.:   CG-92
NAME: Stock Ticker Tape Machine
HEIGHT: 7½"
SLOT: punched in side
INFO: clear glass dome with steel black wrinkle finish bank, paper tape; wing nut bottom trap; Japan
GRADE: D

No.: CG-93
NAME: Save for Victory, Uncle Sam & Lincoln
HEIGHT: 7" x 11"
SLOT: formed in top
INFO: red, white, and blue on light blue; coins drop in top to glass dome; peg holes for marking jobs complete; swing out legs in back for standing; cardboard and glass
GRADE: D

No.: CG-94
NAME: Man in Three Cornered Hat
HEIGHT: 3⅝"
SLOT: converted
INFO: clear glass with slotted metal lid inserted; A Tony Carmi Creation
GRADE: B

No.: CG-95
NAME: My Own Bank, Baby & Dog Looking in Aquarium
HEIGHT: 7" x 11"
SLOT: formed in top
INFO: light blue printed on white; coins drop in top to glass dome; peg holes for marking jobs complete; swing out leg in back for standing
GRADE: D

No.: CG-96
NAME: Medium Souvenir Barrel
HEIGHT: 7⅛"
SLOT: punched in wood top
INFO: Million Dollar Bank, amber glass
GRADE: B

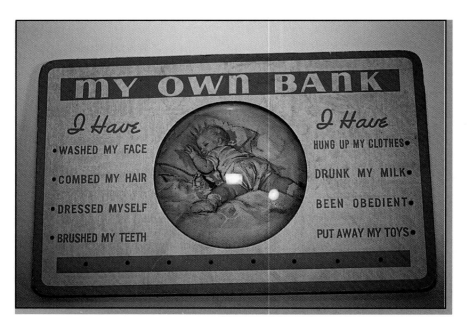

No.: CG-97
NAME: My Own Bank, Baby Sleeping
HEIGHT: 7" x 11"
SLOT: formed in top
INFO: cinnamon brown on white; coins drop in top to glass dome; peg holes for marking jobs complete; swing out leg in back for standing; baby sleeping on stomach, cardboard and glass
GRADE: D

No.: CG-98
NAME: Lantern Design Jar, Noymer
HEIGHT: 7⅛"
SLOT: formed brass slot in top
INFO: clear glass round jar; Money Levels — Long Weekend, Hers, His, Dinner Out; Noymer; leather and glass
GRADE: C

No.: CG-99
NAME: Molson Canadian Beer Imported
HEIGHT: 10¼"
SLOT: cut in top
INFO: paper covered wood with masonite; image screened on inside of glass; Martlet Importing Co. Inc., Great Neck, N.Y.
GRADE: C

No.: CG-100
NAME: Small Souvenir Barrel
HEIGHT: 5½"
SLOT: punched in wood top
INFO: Washington State Capitol — Olympia, amber glass, wood, and brass
GRADE: B

See page 7 for price ranges.

170

No.:   CG-101
NAME: National Cash Register Receipt Box
HEIGHT: 6¼"
SLOT: molded in top
INFO: cast brass on top, bottom, and two sides; two sides
clear glass; often referred to as a bank; key lock top
GRADE: E

No.:   CG-102
NAME: Musical Lantern
HEIGHT: 6½"
SLOT: punched in top
INFO: copper-plated steel bank with medium
amber glass; plays tune when coin is inserted;
bottom trap
GRADE: D

No.:   CG-103
NAME: Giant Bottle
HEIGHT: 19"
SLOT: punched in top
INFO: giant amber
glass bottle bank in
black leather casing with
chain and padlock;
Made in England
GRADE: D

No.:   CG-104
NAME: My Own Bank, Red Riding Hood with Cat
HEIGHT: 7" x 11"
SLOT: formed in top
INFO: light blue printed on white; coins drop in top to glass dome; peg holes for marking jobs complete; swing out leg in back for standing; cardboard and glass
GRADE: D

No.:   CG-105
NAME: Medium Souvenir Barrel
HEIGHT: 7⅛"
SLOT: punched in wood top
INFO: My Winnings From Lake Tahoe, amber glass
GRADE: B

No.:   CG-106
NAME: A Good Turn for the Blind
HEIGHT: 9¾"
SLOT: two slots
INFO: clear glass dome on black steel, wrinkle finished case; cast zinc locking bottom; flat coin slot accepts all coins, raised coin slot accepts large English penny and operates the spinning blind man who points to your fortune; mechanical; England
GRADE: Rare

No.:   CG-107
NAME: Boot
HEIGHT: 6"
SLOT: punched in leather top
INFO: medium blue frosted glass boot with red leather top; found with red or white laces
GRADE: D

RATING/GRADING	
A	To $15.00
B	$15.00 – 35.00
C	$35.00 – 75.00
D	$75.00 – 150.00
E	$150.00 – 300.00
F	$300.00 – 600.00
Rare	$600.00 – 1,000.00
Very Rare	negotiable

NO.: CG-108
NAME: Gettysburg, Pa. Log Slice
HEIGHT: 3⅝"
SLOT: punched in back
INFO: hand-painted scene on tin back; painted scene on flat front glass; Gettysburg, Pa., Savings Bank on front dome glass
GRADE: B

NO.: CG-109
NAME: Lantern
HEIGHT: 5½"
SLOT: punched in top
INFO: light amber glass globe in copper-plated steel lantern; padlock top
GRADE: D

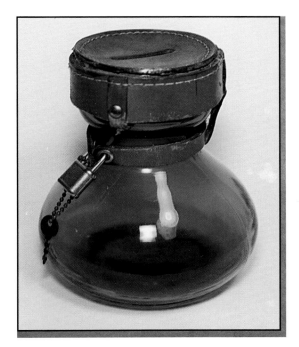

NO.: CG-110
NAME: Muzzled Jar
HEIGHT: 5½"
SLOT: punched in top
INFO: round dark green glass bottle with leather lid and locking straps; padlock top
GRADE: D

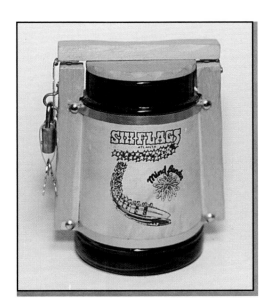

NO.: CG-111
NAME: Small Souvenir Barrel
HEIGHT: 5½"
SLOT: punched in wood top
INFO: Six Flags Atlanta, plastic label bonded to amber glass, wood, and brass
GRADE: B

NO.:   CG-112
NAME: Two Flamingo Log Slice
HEIGHT: 5½"
SLOT: punched in top
INFO: hand-painted scene on tin back; painted scene on flat front glass; Florida Savings Bank on front domed glass
GRADE: D

NO.:   CG-113
NAME: Mickey Mouse Picture Frame
HEIGHT: 9" x 11"
SLOT: punched in top
INFO: tin and clear glass picture; slot in top stores coins behind picture; Label — I'm a Bank
GRADE: C

NO.:   CG-114
NAME: Juggling Circus Clown Music Box
HEIGHT: 5⅞"
SLOT: punched
INFO: musical circus bank plays can-can music and clown dances when coin is inserted; Otagiri
GRADE: C

NO.:   CG-115
NAME: Large Coor's Beer Mug for Bar Tips
HEIGHT: 8¾"
SLOT: formed in foam top
INFO: clear glass with beer color inside, Coor's and Tips in black on outside; plastic foam top with slot; foam comes out to retrieve coins
GRADE: C

NO.: CG-116
NAME: My Own Bank, Baby Peek-a-Boo, Rabbit, and Bottle
HEIGHT: 7" x 11"
SLOT: formed in top
INFO: pink printed on white; coins drop in top to glass dome; peg holes for marking jobs complete; swing out leg in back for standing
GRADE: D

NO.: CG-117
NAME: H.J. Heinz
HEIGHT: 4½"
SLOT: punched in top
INFO: glass H.J. Heinz jar with all brass construction; painted white under edge of two horizontal flat surfaces
GRADE: Very Rare

NO.: CG-118
NAME: Erie, Pennsylvania, Souvenir Jar
HEIGHT: 3½"
SLOT: punched in lid
INFO: leather covered jar bank, plastic photo label
GRADE: C

NO.: CG-119
NAME: Roman Picture
HEIGHT: 6¾"
SLOT: cut in top
INFO: wooden picture frame bank with tin back; church collection?
GRADE: B

NO.: CG-120
NAME: Dutch Hour Glass
HEIGHT: 11¾"
SLOT: punched in top
INFO: wooden framed hour glass with tin top trap and padlock, plastic
GRADE: D

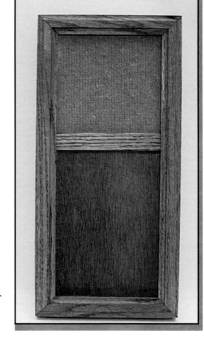

NO.: CG-121
NAME: Needle-point Picture Frame
HEIGHT: 13½"
SLOT: cut in top
INFO: oak frame with glass compartment for a bank
GRADE: B

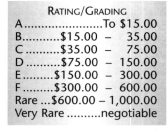

RATING/GRADING	
A	To $15.00
B	$15.00 – 35.00
C	$35.00 – 75.00
D	$75.00 – 150.00
E	$150.00 – 300.00
F	$300.00 – 600.00
Rare	$600.00 – 1,000.00
Very Rare	negotiable

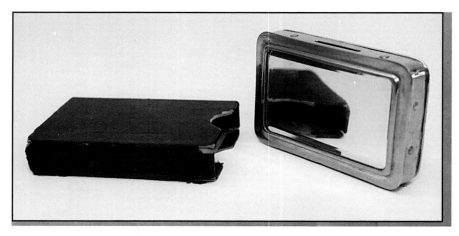

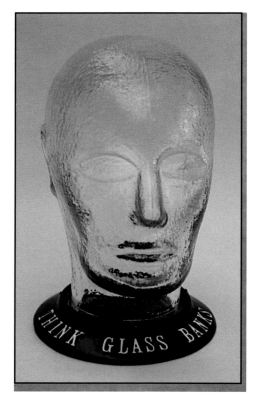

NO.: CG-122
NAME: Vanity Fair Mirror with Slip Case
HEIGHT: 2¼"
SLOT: punched in top edge
INFO: beveled glass mirror in plated steel key lock case; Mfd. by The Bankers Savings & Credit System Co., Cleveland, Ohio; First State Bank, Cambridge, Minn.
GRADE: B

NO.: CG-123
NAME: Think
HEIGHT: 8½"
SLOT: cut in top
INFO: glass head in cast aluminum base
GRADE: E

No.:   CG-124
NAME: Absolut Vodka Mirror Picture
HEIGHT: 10⅛"
SLOT: punched in top edge
INFO: bar advertising mirror bank, Drop Coins and
Bills thru top, "Thank You," tin frame with cardboard
back; Imported by Carillon Importers Ltd., New York
GRADE: C

No.:   CG-125
NAME: Faux Marble Post Office Box
HEIGHT: 5¾"
SLOT: cut in top
INFO: faux marble case with double dial
GRADE: B

No.:   CG-126
NAME: Girl in Bonnet Picture
HEIGHT: 12⅛"
SLOT: cut in top edge
Info: cut out girl in bonnet behind glass with wooden frame
and back, back unscrews; A & W Woodworks, 4300 Willis
Ave., Pennsauken, NJ, 11-1-89, Pat. Pend. 06441674
GRADE: B

No.:   CG-127
NAME: Our Bank — His & Hers
HEIGHT: 7⅝"
SLOT: cut in top edge
INFO: oak and glass with two slots but all money goes in Hers;
gold and black metallic label; His and Hers screened on glass;
rubber plug trap
GRADE: B

Blown Glass Banks

No.: BG-1
NAME: Ball
HEIGHT: 3"
SLOT: stretch molded
INFO: aqua blue; from L.C. Hegarty collection
GRADE: D

No.: BG-2
NAME: Cylinder on Fused Base
HEIGHT: 5¼"
SLOT: stretch molded
INFO: clear glass; from L.C. Hegarty collection
GRADE: D

No.: BG-3
NAME: Red Ball
HEIGHT: 5"
SLOT: stretch molded
INFO: artist: R.F. Holcombe
GRADE: C

No.: BG-4
NAME: Oval Ball
HEIGHT: 4⅝"
SLOT: stretch molded
INFO: dark green glass; artist: R.F. Holcombe
GRADE: C

RATING/GRADING	
A	To $15.00
B	$15.00 – 35.00
C	$35.00 – 75.00
D	$75.00 – 150.00
E	$150.00 – 300.00
F	$300.00 – 600.00
Rare	$600.00 – 1,000.00
Very Rare	negotiable

No.: BG-5
NAME: Pig
Height: 6"
SLOT: stretch molded
INFO: blown purple glass body with clear glass ears, eyes, nose, legs, and tail applied; artist: Bob Rigg, Seattle, Wash.
GRADE: D

NO.: BG-6
NAME: Vase
HEIGHT: 5"
SLOT: stretch molded
INFO: glass striated blue and
clear; artist: Tommy Lockhart,
Columbia, S.C.
Grade: C

NO.: BG-7
NAME: Ball on Base with Lion Heads
HEIGHT: 4⅜"
SLOT: stretch molded
INFO: clear glass
GRADE: D

NO.: BG-8
NAME: Sandwich Glass Early
Reproduction
HEIGHT: 12"
SLOT: stretch molded
INFO: clear glass; sold in Sandwich
Glass Museum shop, 1980s
GRADE: E

NO.: BG-9
NAME: Cinderella's Coach
HEIGHT: 4¼"
SLOT: stretch molded
INFO: clear glass
GRADE: C

NO.: BG-10
NAME: Apple
Height: 4"
SLOT: stretch molded in bottom
INFO: clear; European Penny Bank Club
favor; Royal Leerdam Hand Made
Superieur 30%; Made in Holland
GRADE: D

NO.: BG-11
NAME: Pig
HEIGHT: 6¼"
SLOT: raised stretch formed
INFO: red glass body with clear glass ears, eyes, nose, legs, and tail applied; Bob Rigg, Seattle, Washington
GRADE: D

NO.: BG-12
NAME: Pig
HEIGHT: 4"
SLOT: stretch molded in top
INFO: clear thin glass, hand blown; Christmas 1975, Joyce Riegner
GRADE: D

NO.: BG-13
NAME: Vase
HEIGHT: 4⅞"
SLOT: stretch molded
INFO: dark aqua in twist molded pattern; ART, Czech Republic
GRADE: C

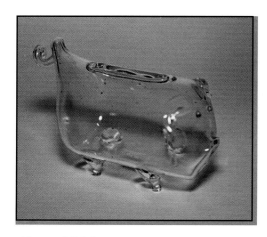

NO.: BG-14
NAME: Pig
HEIGHT: 2⅞"
SLOT: stretch molded in top
INFO: clear glass with applied features, legs, and tail; small, thin
GRADE: C

No.:   BG-15
NAME: Bride's Bank
HEIGHT: 5¾"
SLOT: many openings in top
INFO: clear glass with applied silver design to base; South Jersey style
GRADE: D

No.:   BG-16
NAME: Rosenthal Heart Vase
HEIGHT: 3½"
SLOT: stretch molded
INFO: clear glass with Rosenthal clear plastic label; Rosenthal etched in bottom; Made in Brazil sticker
GRADE: C

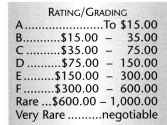

RATING/GRADING	
A	To $15.00
B	$15.00 – 35.00
C	$35.00 – 75.00
D	$75.00 – 150.00
E	$150.00 – 300.00
F	$300.00 – 600.00
Rare	$600.00 – 1,000.00
Very Rare	negotiable

No.:   BG-17
NAME: Bride's Bank
HEIGHT: 5"
SLOT: many openings in top
INFO: clear glass with amber glass middle edge; South Jersey style
GRADE: D

No.:   BG-18
NAME: Bride's Bank
HEIGHT: 3¼"
SLOT: many openings in top
INFO: clear glass; South Jersey style
GRADE: D

No.:   BG-19
NAME: Bride's Bank
HEIGHT: 8⅝"
SLOT: many openings in top
INFO: clear glass with applied silver design to base; South Jersey style
GRADE: D

No.: BG-20
NAME: Bride's Bank
HEIGHT: 6"
SLOT: many openings in top
INFO: clear glass; double fluted bottom design
GRADE: D

No.: BG-21
NAME: Bride's Bank
HEIGHT: 6"
SLOT: many openings in top
INFO: clear glass; South Jersey style
GRADE: D

No.: BG-22
NAME: Bride's Bank
HEIGHT: 4½"
SLOT: many openings in top
INFO: silvered top openings with clear glass base
GRADE: D

No.: BG-23
NAME: Bride's Bank
HEIGHT: 4⅛"
SLOT: many openings in top
INFO: clear glass; South Jersey style
GRADE: D

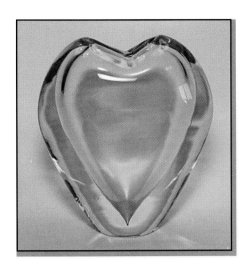

No.:   BG-24
NAME: Heart
HEIGHT: 5⅛"
SLOT: stretch molded
INFO: clear glass, thick, heavy
GRADE: C

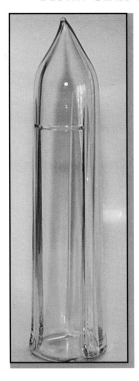

No.:   BG-25
NAME: Monument
HEIGHT: 14"
SLOT: cut in side
INFO: clear glass, thick-walled with vertical flutes in glass bottom fused closed
GRADE: D

No.:   BG-26
NAME: Pig's Head
HEIGHT: 5⅝"
SLOT: stretch molded in top
INFO: red glass head with clear glass ears, eyes, nose, and tail applied
GRADE: D

No.:   BG-27
NAME: Elephant's Head
HEIGHT: 6¾"
SLOT: cut in top
INFO: large; smoke glass head with clear glass ears, eyes, trunk, and tusks applied; open bottom with cardboard closure
GRADE: D

No.:   BG-28
NAME: Muuria Oval
HEIGHT: 3⅝"
SLOT: stretch molded in top
INFO: clear glass with blues, white, and browns mixed; Muuria, Finland
GRADE: D

No.: BG-29
NAME: Ball
HEIGHT: 4¼"
SLOT: stretch molded
INFO: cobalt blue glass ball with fluted collar neck; artist: Garth Mudge, Estes Park, Colorado
GRADE: C

No.: BG-32
NAME: Bent Neck with Open Spout
HEIGHT: 8"
SLOT: stretch molded
INFO: blue, silver, red, and gold variegated glass; artist: Mountain Lake Glassworks, Tracy City, Tennessee
GRADE: C

No.: BG-30
NAME: Bent Neck with Pointed Opening
HEIGHT: 9¾"
SLOT: stretch molded
INFO: blue and clear glass with gold variegated stripes; artist: Mountain Lake Glassworks, Tracy City, Tennessee
GRADE: C

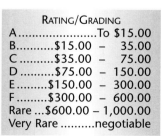

RATING/GRADING	
A	To $15.00
B	$15.00 – 35.00
C	$35.00 – 75.00
D	$75.00 – 150.00
E	$150.00 – 300.00
F	$300.00 – 600.00
Rare	$600.00 – 1,000.00
Very Rare	negotiable

No.: BG-31
NAME: Variegated Ball
HEIGHT: 4¼"
SLOT: stretch molded
INFO: variegated blue and white ball with fluted collar neck; artist: Garth Mudge, Estes Park, Colorado
GRADE: C

No.: BG-33
NAME: Oval on Fluted Base
HEIGHT: 6"
SLOT: stretch molded
INFO: dark red glass; artist: Glassworks Gallery, Sperryville, Virginia
GRADE: C

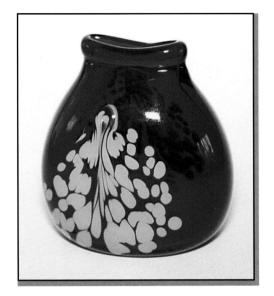

No.: BG-34
NAME: Oval
HEIGHT: 5¼"
SLOT: stretch molded
INFO: cobalt blue glass with orange design;
artist: Glassworks Gallery, Sperryville, Virginia
Grade: C

No.: BG-35
NAME: Stylized Frog
HEIGHT: 6¾"
SLOT: stretch molded
INFO: green with clear glass;
gold overlay; artist: Mountain Lake
Glassworks, Tracy City, Tennessee
GRADE: C

No.: BG-36
NAME: Heavy Vase
HEIGHT: 6"
SLOT: stretch molded
INFO: clear with green glass, red dot design;
artist: Glassworks Gallery, Sperryville, Virginia
GRADE: C

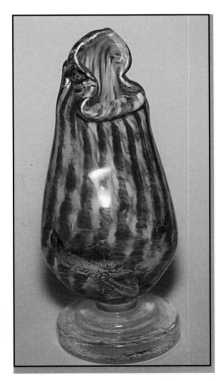

No.: BG-37
NAME: Pedestal Vase
HEIGHT: 8"
SLOT: stretch molded
INFO: blue and clear glass with
gold overlay; fluted mouth; artist:
Mountain Lake Glassworks, Tracy
City, Tennessee
GRADE: C

Fabricated Glass Banks

NO.:   FG-1
NAME: U.S. Depository Bank, Jan. 29, 1892
HEIGHT: 6"
SLOT: formed in tin chimney
INFO: unique handmade glass walls in tin frame with tin roof and floor; hand-painted windows and doors, lettering in black, gold, and blue; roof originally covered in a fabric
GRADE: Rare

RATING/GRADING	
A	To $15.00
B	$15.00 – 35.00
C	$35.00 – 75.00
D	$75.00 – 150.00
E	$150.00 – 300.00
F	$300.00 – 600.00
Rare	$600.00 – 1,000.00
Very Rare	negotiable

NO.:   FG-2
NAME: Plain House
HEIGHT: 3¾"
SLOT: formed in roof peak
INFO: red, green, and clear glass leaded together; a Burton VanAsdale Creation
GRADE: B

No.:   FG-3
NAME: Jesus Saves
HEIGHT: 4⅝"
SLOT: punched in top
INFO: pictures printed on clear glass, leaded in tin frame; Mexico, Tesoros
Grade: C

No.:   FG-4
NAME: Stained Glass Kit
HEIGHT: 8¾"
SLOT: cut in top
INFO: oak case with patterns for seven stained glass designs; stained glass on both sides; Clarity #145
Grade: C

No.:   FG-5
NAME: Independence Hall
HEIGHT: 10⅛" x 14⅝"
SLOT: in back of center tower
INFO: made of red, blue, white, and clear glass leaded together; some pieces are formed brass; leather interior floor where coins drop; trap is a spring clasp closure; walnut base with felt bottom; 200 hours construction; 1989, Charles Steeber
GRADE: F

Candy Container Banks

No.: CC-1
Name: Independence Hall
Height: 7½"
Slot: punch out in roof
Info: earliest version; clear glass with no design on interior ceiling; bottom formed to fit wooden base as described in patent papers; wooden base frame with slide-out trap is held by small screw
Grade: Very Rare

No.: CC-2
Name: Independence Hall
Height: 7¼"
Slot: punch out in roof
Info: clear glass with square and rectangular patterns molded on interior ceiling; Bank of Independence Hall, 1776 – 1876 over front door, Patent Pending over back door; slide-on tin closure
Grade: F

PHOTO NOT AVAILABLE
No.: CC-4
Name: Independence Hall
Height: 7½"
Slot: punch out in roof
Info: milk glass with same markings as later version; slide-on tin closure
Grade: Rare

No.: CC-3
Name: Boston Kettle Defense Stamps
Height: 2⅛"
Slot: punched out in cardboard
Info: clear glass three-leg pot with bottom painted brown; paper handle; closure is cardboard; this Boston kettle filled with dimes will buy $10 worth of Defense Stamps; T.H. Stough Co., Jeannette, Pa.
Grade: E

NO.: CC-5
NAME: Small Independence Hall
HEIGHT: 5¼"
SLOT: punch out in roof
INFO: clear glass with tower molded on side of building; cardboard and red felt bottom glued on inside bottom; made in 1976
GRADE: C

NO.: CC-6
NAME: Dome or Planetarium
HEIGHT: 4⅛"
SLOT: molded in top
INFO: clear glass round building with stars; tin screw on closure; called Dome Bank in 1887 McKee and Bros. catalog
GRADE: F

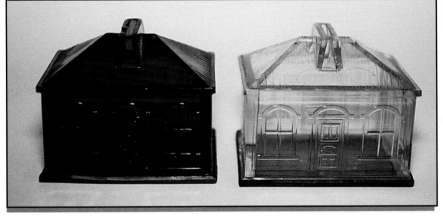

NO.: CC-7
NAME: Cabinet House
HEIGHT: 3⅛"
SLOT: molded in chimney
INFO: clear, green, or dark amber glass house with center chimney; tin bottom crimped on four sides; called Cabinet Bank in 1887 McKee and Bros. catalog
GRADE: E

RATING/GRADING	
A	To $15.00
B	$15.00 – 35.00
C	$35.00 – 75.00
D	$75.00 – 150.00
E	$150.00 – 300.00
F	$300.00 – 600.00
Rare	$600.00 – 1,000.00
Very Rare	negotiable

NO.: CC-8
NAME: Liberty Bell
HEIGHT: 4⅜"
SLOT: punch out in top
INFO: clear glass with molded double crack and Liberty, 1776; Hanger — Pat. Applied For; Bottom — tin screw on, embossed; Robinson & Loeble, 723 Wharton St., Phila, Pa.
GRADE: E

No.: CC-9
Name: Liberty Bell
Height: 4⅜"
Slot: punch out in top
Info: amber glass with molded single crack and Liberty, 1776; Hanger — Pat. Applied For or Patented Sept. 22, 1885; Bottom — tin, screw on, embossed; Robinson & Loeble, 723 Wharton St., Phila., Pa.
Grade: D

No.: CC-10
Name: Liberty Bell
Height: 4⅜"
Slot: punch out in top
Info: milk glass with molded single crack and Liberty, 1776; Hanger — Patented Sept. 22, 1885; Bottom — tin, screw on, embossed; Robinson & Loeble, 723 Wharton St., Phila., Pa.
Grade: D

No.: CC-11
Name: Liberty Bell
Height: 4⅜"
Slot: punch out in top
Info: blue glass with molded single crack and Liberty, 1776; Hanger — Patented Sept. 22, 1885; Bottom — tin, screw on, embossed; Robinson & Loeble, 723 Wharton St., Phila., Pa.
Grade: D

No.: CC-12
Name: Small Liberty Bell
Height: 2⅜"
Slot: punch out in cardboard top
Info: clear glass with 1776 on one side, and Pass and Stow, Philada, MDCCLIII, on the other; Lid — red, white, and blue tin litho with 16 stars, center of lid punched out in circle, lid liner shows pre-marked slot
Grade: E

No.: CC-13
Name: Mail Box
Height: 3¼"
Slot: punched and non-slotted
Info: clear painted glass, painted silver with black letters and trim; back of bank is completely flat; reproduction has rectangle molded at the bottom of the back side; tin slide-on slotted closure
Grade: E

No.: CC-15
Name: Uncle Sam Hat
Height: 2"
Slot: punched in top
Info: milk glass with red, blue, and gold painted areas; press-in tin slotted closure with paper label showing Republican nominees Taft and Sherman
Grade: E

No.: CC-14
Name: Drum Mug
Height: 2½"
Slot: punched in top
Info: milk glass with red, blue, and gold painted areas; press-in original slotted closure made of tin
Grade: E

RATING/GRADING	
A	To $15.00
B	$15.00 – 35.00
C	$35.00 – 75.00
D	$75.00 – 150.00
E	$150.00 – 300.00
F	$300.00 – 600.00
Rare	$600.00 – 1,000.00
Very Rare	negotiable

No.: CC-16
Name: Eagle Drum
Height: 1¾"
Slot: punched in top
Info: milk glass drum with crossed flags and cannons design; painted red and gold or green and gold; tin screw-on embossed closure with Eagle and U.S. Treasury
Grade: F

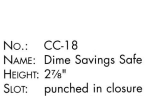

No.: CC-18
Name: Dime Savings Safe
Height: 2⅞"
Slot: punched in closure
Info: clear glass with two rectangular inset panels on all sides; Dime Savings Bank on front; slide-on tin slotted closure painted dark blue
Grade: D

No.: CC-17
Name: Drum Mug
Height: 2½"
Sot: punched in top
Info: clear glass with gold painted areas; press-in slotted lid has been replaced
Grade: C

191

No.:   CC-19
Name: Dime Savings Safe
Height: 2⅞"
Slot: punched in closure
Info: clear glass with two rectangular inset panels on all sides; Dime Savings Bank on front; C.D. Kenny Co. on back; slide-on tin slotted closure
Grade: D

No.:   CC-20
Name: Penny Trust Co. Safe
Height: 2⅞"
Slot: punched in closure
Info: milk glass with gold painted areas; gold slide-on tin slotted closure
Grade: D

No.:   CC-21
Name: Dime Savings Safe
Height: 3⅛"
Slot: non-slotted
Info: clear glass safe bank with clear glass top; made by Westmoreland Glass or in Taiwan, about 1973
Grade: C

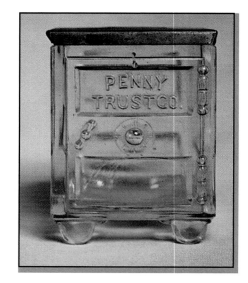

No.:   CC-22
Name: Penny Trust Co. Safe
Height: 2⅞"
Slot: punched in closure
Info: clear glass with two rectangular inset panels on all sides; gold slide-on tin slotted closure
Grade: D

No.:   CC-23
Name: Penny Trust Co. Safe
Height: 2⅞"
Slot: punched in closure
Info: clear glass with ruby flashed areas; Back — flat, no panels, Souvenir of York, Pa.; slotted, plain tin closure
Grade: E

No.: CC-24
Name: Penny Trust Co. Safe
HEIGHT: 2⅞"
SLOT: punched in closure
INFO: milk glass, slotted tin closure; three sides with inset panels, flat back with painted sailing ship scene; slotted tin closure, painted white; Brock, Canada
GRADE: E

No.: CC-25
NAME: Penny Trust Co. Safe
HEIGHT: 2⅞"
SLOT: punched in closure
INFO: green glass with three inset side panels and flat back; replaced snap-on tin slotted closure
GRADE: C

No.: CC-26
NAME: Penny Trust Co. Safe
HEIGHT: 3⅛"
SLOT: non-slotted
INFO: vaseline glass top glows under black light; bottom interior floor is ½" thick; made in 1999
GRADE: C

No.: CC-27
NAME: Penny Trust Co. Safe
HEIGHT: 3⅛"
SLOT: non-slotted
INFO: cobalt blue, amber, green, or clear glass; made by Westmoreland Glass Co. in 1973 (shown with vaseline glass safe)
GRADE: C

No.: CC-28
NAME: Candy Pay Station Pay Phone Mechanical
HEIGHT: 5¾"
SLOT: punched in front
INFO: clear glass inside plastic phone; Insert Pennies Only – and you get some candy beads; Save on front bottom, back trap, J.H. Millstein Co., Jeannette, Pa.
GRADE: F

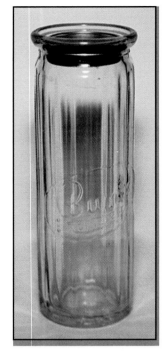

NO.: CC-29
NAME: Bunte Candy Jar
HEIGHT: 4¼"
SLOT: punched in closure
INFO: short, clear glass vertical ribbed jar; press-in copper colored tin slotted lid; thin round glass lid on top of inset tin closure; Bunte–Chicago
GRADE: D

NO.: CC-30
NAME: Bunte Candy Jar
Height: 6"
SLOT: punched in closure
INFO: tall, clear glass vertical ribbed jar; press-in copper colored tin slotted lid; thin round glass lid on top of inset tin closure; Bunte–Chicago
GRADE: D

NO.: CC-31
NAME: Mantel Clock
HEIGHT: 3¾"
SLOT: punched in closure
INFO: clear glass with painted gold trim; paper clock face; slide-on tin slotted closure
GRADE: E

NO.: CC-32
NAME: Mantel Clock
HEIGHT: 3¾"
SLOT: punch out in back
INFO: clear glass with painted gold trim; paper clock face; slide-on tin slotted closure
GRADE: E

NO.: CC-33
NAME: Phonograph with Tin Horn
HEIGHT: 4¼"
SLOT: punched in closure
INFO: clear glass with red rolled tin horn; slide-on tin slotted closure
GRADE: E

RATING/GRADING	
A	To $15.00
B	$15.00 – 35.00
C	$35.00 – 75.00
D	$75.00 – 150.00
E	$150.00 – 300.00
F	$300.00 – 600.00
Rare	$600.00 – 1,000.00
Very Rare	negotiable

No.: CC-34
NAME: Piano
HEIGHT: 2⅞"
SLOT: punched in back closure
INFO: clear glass painted gold, also in ruby flashed or milk glass; flat inset panel in front above pedals; slide-on tin slotted back closure
GRADE: E

No.: CC-35
NAME: Goblin Head
HEIGHT: 3⅝"
SLOT: punched in bottom closure
INFO: clear glass with orange, green, black, white, and red; screw-on yellow slotted tin bottom closure
GRADE: Rare

No.: CC-36
NAME: Octagonal Clock
HEIGHT: 3⅞"
SLOT: punched in back closure
INFO: clear glass octagonal clock found in red or green; paper clock face; screw-on yellow tin slotted closure
GRADE: E

No.: CC-37
NAME: Barney Google on Pedestal
HEIGHT: 3⅞"
SLOT: punched and non-slotted
INFO: clear glass Barney Google on front of base; painted figure; screw-on tin slotted closure
GRADE: F

No.: CC-38
NAME: Kewpie
HEIGHT: 3³⁄₁₆"
SLOT: punched in closure
INFO: clear glass with painted Kewpie; twist-on tin litho woodgrain closure; Borgfelt & Co. N.Y.
GRADE: D

NO.: CC-39
NAME: Skookum by Tree Stump
HEIGHT: 3⅝"
SLOT: punched in closure
INFO: clear glass with painted figure and tree stump; Skookum on front of base; twist-on slotted tin closure, lithographed to look like rings on top of tree stump; Borgfelt & Co. N.Y.
GRADE: Rare

NO.: CC-40
NAME: Charlie Chaplin by Curved Barrel
HEIGHT: 3¾"
SLOT: punched in closure
INFO: clear glass with Charlie Chaplin on base front, painted figure; twist-on slotted tin closure lithographed in woodgrain pattern; Borgfelt & Co. N.Y.
GRADE: D

NO.: CC-41
NAME: Charlie Chaplin by Straight Barrel Bank
HEIGHT: 4¹⁄₁₆"
SLOT: punched in closure
INFO: clear glass with painted figure (glass cane top usually broken off); yellow or plain screw-on tin slotted closure; L.E. Smith Co., Net. Wt. 1½ oz.
GRADE: Rare

NO.: CC-42
NAME: Safety First Baby by Barrel
HEIGHT: 3¾"
SLOT: punched in closure
INFO: clear glass, Safety First on base front, painted figure; yellor or orange screw-on tin slotted closure; West Bros. (not marked)
GRADE: F

No.: CC-43
Name: Santa Claus by Square Chimney
Height: 3⅝"
Slot: punched in closure
Info: clear glass with Santa painted red or green with white, orange, and gold trim; gold or red slide-on tin slotted closure; L.E. Smith Co. (not marked)
Grade: F

No.: CC-44
Name: Happifats on Drum
Height: 4½"
Slot: punched in bottom closure
Info: clear glass, painted figure and drum top; tin slotted twist on closure stamped Geo. Borgfelt & Co., N.Y.
Grade: F

No.: CC-45
Name: Baseball Player by Barrel
Height: 3¼"
Slot: punched in closure
Info: clear glass with painted figure; orange or yellow tin screw-on slotted closure
Grade: Rare

No.: CC-46
Name: Uncle Sam by Barrel
Height: 3⅞"
Slot: punched in closure
Info: clear glass with painted figure; orange or yellow tin screw-on slotted closure
Grade: Rare

No.: CC-47
NAME: Pop-eyed Jack O'Lantern
HEIGHT: 2½"
SLOT: punched in lid
INFO: clear glass painted orange, black, red, and white; screw-on tin slotted closure; steel wire bail handle
GRADE: Rare

No.: CC-48
NAME: Felix by Barrel
HEIGHT: 3⁷⁄₁₆"
SLOT: punched in closure
INFO: clear glass with Felix on barrel; tin slotted tab on red closure; copyright 1922 – 24, by Pat Sullivan, Pat. Applied For
GRADE: Rare

No.: CC-49
NAME: Lynne Clock Bank
HEIGHT: 4¹³⁄₁₆"
SLOT: punched in tin clock top
INFO: clear glass base with litho tin clock top; J.C. Crosetti Co., Jeannette, Pa.
GRADE: Rare

No.: CC-50
NAME: Barney Google by Barrel
HEIGHT: 3⅛"
SLOT: punched in closure
INFO: clear glass with Barney Google on barrel front; orange or yellow tin screw-on slotted closure
GRADE: Very Rare

No.: CC-51
NAME: Dog by Barrel
HEIGHT: 3⅛"
SLOT: punched in closure
INFO: clear glass with painted figure, some dogs with amber bead eyes; orange or yellow tin screw-on slotted closure; L.E. Smith Co.
GRADE: E

No.: CC-52
NAME: Rabbit with Forepaws
Next to Body
HEIGHT: 5 1/16"
SLOT: punched in closure
INFO: clear glass with top
of rabbit painted gold; tin
screw-on slotted closure
GRADE: D

No.: CC-53
NAME: Santa Claus in Banded
Coat
Height: 5 1/8"
SLOT: punched in closure
INFO: clear glass painted
from top down to coat bottom
and leg fronts; tin screw-on
slotted closure
GRADE: E

No.: CC-54
NAME: Rabbit with Feet
Together
HEIGHT: 5 3/16"
SLOT: punched in closure
INFO: clear glass or painted
gold; tin screw-on slotted closure
GRADE: D

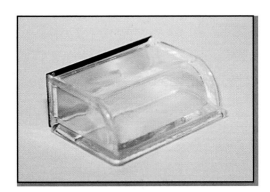

No.: CC-55
NAME: Glass Display Case
HEIGHT: 1 9/16"
SLOT: punched in closure; conversion
INFO: clear glass reproduction with new tin
slotted black closure; Serial No. 2862, Net
Wt. 1 1/4 oz., Pat. Apl'd For, West Bros. mold
GRADE: D

RATING/GRADING	
A	To $15.00
B	$15.00 – 35.00
C	$35.00 – 75.00
D	$75.00 – 150.00
E	$150.00 – 300.00
F	$300.00 – 600.00
Rare	$600.00 – 1,000.00
Very Rare	negotiable

No.: CC-56
NAME: Kangaroo Conversion
HEIGHT: 5 3/8"
SLOT: cut in glass front
INFO: clear glass with slot
cut in front of animal after mar-
ket; screw-on tin closure
GRADE: Rare

No.: CC-58
NAME: Arch-Top Clock
HEIGHT: 3¼"
SLOT: punched in closure
INFO: clear, green, or cobalt blue glass; remade by Westmoreland Glass in 1973; plain tin slotted closure
GRADE: D

No.: CC-57
NAME: Rabbit in Eggshell
HEIGHT: 5¼"
SLOT: punched in closure
INFO: clear glass with painted gold rabbit; AVOIR 1 oz., USA; tin screw-on slotted closure
GRADE: D

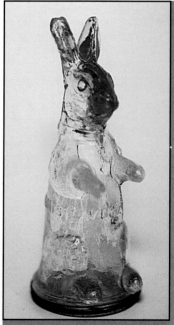

No.: CC-59
NAME: Small Stein
HEIGHT: 2¾"
SLOT: punched in lid
INFO: clear glass with D.R.G.M. on bottom; tin hinged lid with lock, eagle with laurel leaves on lid
GRADE: E

No.: CC-60
NAME: Medium Stein
HEIGHT: 3"
SLOT: punched in lid
INFO: clear glass with D.R.G.M. on bottom; tin hinged lid with lock
GRADE: E

No.: CC-61
NAME: Large Stein
HEIGHT: 4"
SLOT: punched in lid
INFO: clear glass with D.R.G.M. on bottom; tin hinged lid with lock
GRADE: E

No.: CC-62
NAME: Rabbit with Legs Apart
HEIGHT: 5½"
SLOT: punched in closure
INFO: clear glass with head painted red or green; Contents 1¾ AVD oz.; tin screw-on slotted closure
GRADE: E

NO.: CC-63
NAME: Bulldog with Round Base
HEIGHT: 4¹⁄₁₆"
SLOT: punched in closure
INFO: clear glass painted black or
brown with silver or gold collar;
U.S.A. between legs; screw-on tin
slotted closure
GRADE: D

NO.: CC-64
NAME: Merry Christmas Mug
HEIGHT: 3"
SLOT: punched in closure
INFO: opal glass with hand-painted
flower and stamped Merry Christmas;
press-on slotted closure
GRADE: D

NO.: CC-65
NAME: Three-handled Trophy Cup
HEIGHT: 3½"
SLOT: punched
INFO: clear glass with gold painted
areas; closure is round tin slotted tab on
conversion
GRADE: B

NO.: CC-66
NAME: Victory Mug
HEIGHT: 4⅛"
SLOT: punched in lid
INFO: clear glass with vertical rib pat-
tern; screw-on tin slotted lid; conversion?
GRADE: C

NO.: CC-67
NAME: Sitting Hound Dog
HEIGHT: 3⅝"
SLOT: punched in lid
INFO: clear glass; screw-on
tin slotted closure
GRADE: C

NO.: CC-68
NAME: Owl
Height: 4⁷⁄₁₆"
SLOT: punched in closure
INFO: clear glass painted
brown or black; screw-on tin
slotted closure
GRADE: F

NO.: CC-69
NAME: Two-handled Trophy Cup
HEIGHT: 3⅝"
SLOT: punched in closure
INFO: opal glass painted gold; snap-on tin slotted lid; conversion; Farmers Savings Bank, South English, Iowa
GRADE: D

NO.: CC-70
NAME: West Limousine
HEIGHT: 2⅝"
SLOT: punched in roof
INFO: clear glass, red tin wheels, steel axles, black tin slotted slide-on roof closure; West Bros. Co., Grapeville, Pa, Serial No. 2882, Net Wt. 1¼ oz., Pat. Apld For
GRADE: Rare

RATING/GRADING	
A	To $15.00
B	$15.00 – 35.00
C	$35.00 – 75.00
D	$75.00 – 150.00
E	$150.00 – 300.00
F	$300.00 – 600.00
Rare	$600.00 – 1,000.00
Very Rare	negotiable

NO.: CC-71
NAME: Village Church
HEIGHT: 3½"
SLOT: punched in roof
INFO: tin litho church and steeple with plain black slotted roof; steeple holds a ⅜" high glass cross painted gold (missing); clear glass liner inside with wire retainer on bottom
GRADE: Very Rare

NO.: CC-72
NAME: Dog in the Dog House
HEIGHT: 2⅝"
SLOT: punched in tin roof
INFO: milk glass painted gold, green, and black; tin slotted slide-on roof closure
GRADE: F

NO.: CC-73
NAME: Hen on Nest
HEIGHT: 6"
SLOT: molded in side
INFO: bright blue, olive green, light emerald green, or golden amber glass; blue or yellow oval plastic snap-on closure; Crownford China Co. Inc., N.Y.; Italy, 1966
GRADE: D

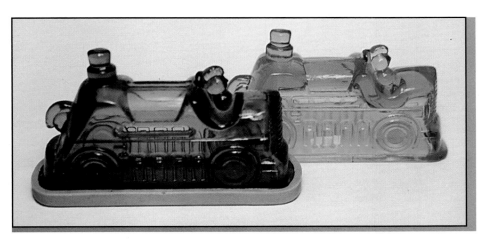

NO.: CC-74
NAME: Firetruck
HEIGHT: 3⅛"
SLOT: molded in side
INFO: bright blue, olive green, light emerald green, or golden amber glass; blue or yellow oval plastic snap-on closure; Cranford China Co. Inc., N.Y.; Italy, 1966
GRADE: D

NO.: CC-75
NAME: Sitting Rabbit
HEIGHT: 6⅛"
SLOT: molded in back of rabbit
INFO: bright blue, olive green, light emerald green, or golden amber glass; blue or yellow oval plastic snap-on closure; Cranford China Co. Inc., N.Y.; Italy, 1966
GRADE: D

NO.: CC-76
NAME: Locomotive 1028
HEIGHT: 3¼"
SLOT: molded in side
INFO: bright blue, olive green, light emerald green, or golden amber glass; blue or yellow oval plastic snap-on closure; Cranford China Co. Inc., N.Y; Italy, 1966.
GRADE: D

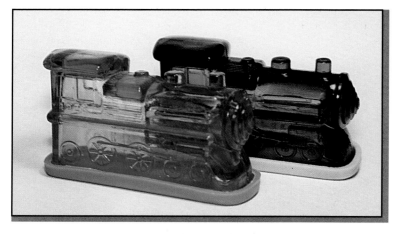

NO.: CC-77
NAME: Piano
HEIGHT: 2⅞"
SLOT: punched in closure
INFO: Westmoreland Glass in amethyst or cobalt blue; Taiwan (marked on bottom) in clear, cobalt, brown, or green; plain tin slide-on slotted closure; 1973
GRADE: C

No.: CC-78
NAME: Dog in the Dog House Reproduction
HEIGHT: 2⅝"
SLOT: punched in tin roof
INFO: milk glass, blue carnival glass, or purple slag glass; gold tin slide-on slotted roof closure; Taiwan, 1998
GRADE: C

RATING/GRADING	
A	To $15.00
B	$15.00 – 35.00
C	$35.00 – 75.00
D	$75.00 – 150.00
E	$150.00 – 300.00
F	$300.00 – 600.00
Rare	$600.00 – 1,000.00
Very Rare	negotiable

No.: CC-79
NAME: Mailbox
HEIGHT: 3¼"
SLOT: punched in closure
INFO: light blue, clear, amber, green, or cobalt blue glass (rectangle molded out on back bottom of bank); Westmoreland and Taiwan, 1973, Taiwan pieces marked on bottom
GRADE: C

Glass Bubble Banks

No.: BB-1
NAME: Chicken Feed
HEIGHT: 6½"
SLOT: raised slot
INFO: chicken facing left; Bottom label — see variation #2; Back of figure — thermometer money meter
GRADE: D

No.: BB-2
NAME: Chicken Feed
HEIGHT: 6½"
SLOT: raised slot
INFO: chicken facing forward; Bottom label — see variation #3; Back of figure — thermometer money meter
GRADE: D

Vic Moran Bubble Banks
Bradford, Pennsylvania
First patent date January 14, 1941

VARIATION INFORMATION
Glass Bubble Globes
A. completely round base bottom
B. three small notches in base bottom
C. slots
    raised, cut off
    raised, polished smooth
    many with roughness to slot

Wooden Bases
A. two-part base with slot cut in middle for cardboard figure; three screws
B. one-piece wood with slot cut off-center; two or three screws
C. one-piece wood with larger holes for three black rubber balls to attach bubble to base

Cardboard Figure Back Sides
A. plain white
B. same as front image printed in reverse
C. thermometer money meter

Base Finishes
A. painted with contrasting silk-screened lettering
B. clear finish with red silk-screened lettering

See bottom labels on page 215.

No.: BB-3
NAME: Chicken Feed
HEIGHT: 6½"
SLOT: raised slot
INFO: red, white, and blue chicken; Bottom label — see variation #1; Back of figure — same figure printed in reverse
GRADE: D

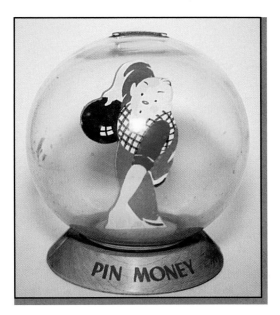

NO.: BB-4
NAME: Man Bowling for Pin Money
HEIGHT: 6½"
SLOT: raised slot
INFO: Bottom label — see variation #1; Back
of figure — same figure printed in reverse
GRADE: E

NO.: BB-5
NAME: Snowman with Broom
HEIGHT: 6½"
SLOT: raised slot
INFO: Bottom label — see variation #1; Back of fig-
ure — same figure printed in reverse
GRADE: Very Rare

See page 7 for price ranges.

NO.: BB-6
NAME: Man snd Woman Bowling for Pin
Money
HEIGHT: 6½"
SLOT: raised slot
INFO: Bottom label — see variation #5; Back
of figure — thermometer money meter
GRADE: E

NO.: BB-7
NAME: A Little Doe
HEIGHT: 6½"
SLOT: raised slot
INFO: deer with bow tie, facing left; Bottom label — see
variation #4; Back of figure — thermometer money meter
GRADE: D

NO.: BB-8
NAME: A Little Doe
HEIGHT: 6½"
SLOT: raised slot
INFO: yellow or tan deer; Bottom label — see variation #3; Back of figure — thermometer money meter
GRADE: D

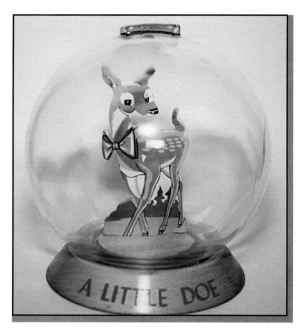

NO.: BB-9
NAME: A Little Doe
HEIGHT: 6½"
SLOT: raised slot
INFO: deer with large bow tie, facing right; Bottom label — see variation #5; Back of figure — thermometer money meter
GRADE: D

NO.: BB-10
NAME: Moo-La
HEIGHT: 6½"
SLOT: raised slot
INFO: cow with bell; Bottom label — see variation #4; Back of figure — thermometer money meter
GRADE: D

NO.: BB-11
NAME: You Can Bank on America
HEIGHT: 6½"
SLOT: raised slot
INFO: two servicemen; Bottom label — see variation #5; Back of figure — thermometer money meter
GRADE: F

No.: BB-12
Name: Drop It in the Trunk Elephant
Height: 6½"
Slot: raised slot
Info: Bottom label — see variation #5; Back of figure — thermometer money meter
Grade: E

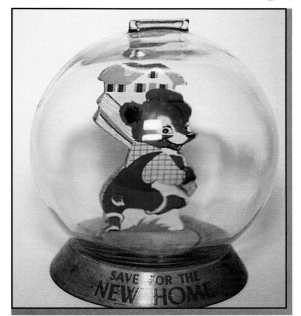

No.: BB-13
Name: Save for the New Home
Height: 6½"
Slot: raised slot
Info: bear with lumber and a house; Bottom label — see variation #5; Back of figure — thermometer money meter
Grade: E

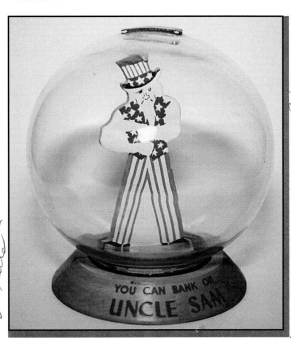

No.: BB-14
Name: You Can Bank on Uncle Sam
Height: 6½"
Slot: raised slot
Info: Uncle Sam rolling sleeves; Bottom label — see variation #1; Back of figure — same figure printed in reverse
Grade: Very Rare

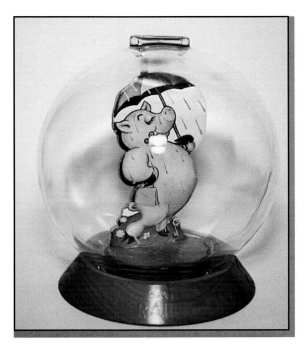

No.: BB-15
Name: Save for a Rainy Day
Height: 6½"
Slot: raised slot
Info: pig with umbrella; Bottom label — see variation #4; Back of figure — thermometer money meter
Grade: D

NO.: BB-16
NAME: Change for the New Baby
HEIGHT: 6½"
SLOT: raised slot
INFO: baby with finger in mouth; Bottom label — see variation #4; Back of figure — thermometer money meter
GRADE: D

NO.: BB-17
NAME: Change for the Baby
HEIGHT: 6½"
SLOT: raised slot
INFO: baby with rattle and beads; Bottom label — see variation #5; Back of figure — thermometer money meter
GRADE: D

NO.: BB-18
NAME: Change for the New Baby
HEIGHT: 6½"
SLOT: raised slot
INFO: pink pillow; no bottom label; Back of figure — thermometer money meter; has only two screws
GRADE: E

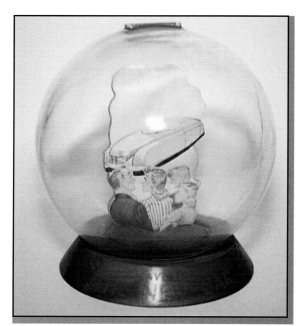

NO.: BB-19
NAME: Save for the New Car
HEIGHT: 6½"
SLOT: raised slot
INFO: family of four with car; Bottom label — see variation #5; Back of figure — thermometer money meter
GRADE: E

NO.:   BB-20
NAME: A Little Jack Rabbit with Carrot
HEIGHT: 6½"
SLOT: raised slot
INFO: Bottom label — see variation #5; Back of figure — thermometer money meter
GRADE: F

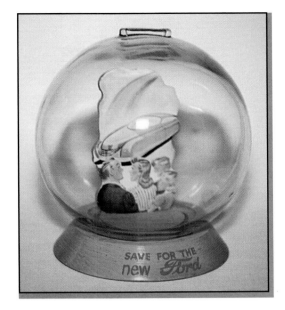

NO.:   BB-21
NAME: Save for the New Ford
HEIGHT: 6½"
SLOT: raised slot
INFO: family of four with car; Bottom label — see variation #4; Back of figure — thermometer money meter
GRADE: F

NO.:   BB-22
NAME: Save for the Kids
HEIGHT: 6½"
SLOT: raised slot
INFO: two yellow goats; Bottom label — see variation #5; Back of figure — thermometer money meter
GRADE: F

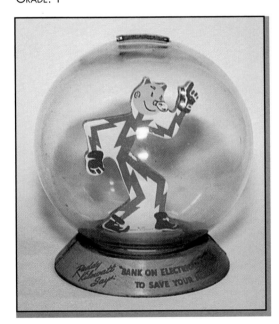

NO.:   BB-23
NAME: Reddy Kilowatt Says
HEIGHT: 6½"
SLOT: raised slot
INFO: Bottom label — see variation #5; Back of figure — same figure printed in reverse
GRADE: Rare

See page 7 for price ranges.

No.: BB-24
NAME: Save for the Kids
HEIGHT: 6½"
SLOT: raised slot
INFO: gray and tan goats; Bottom label — see variation #4; Back of figure — thermometer money meter
GRADE: F

No.: BB-25
NAME: Stop Monkeying and Start Saving
HEIGHT: 6½"
SLOT: raised slot
INFO: monkey wearing vest; Bottom label — see variation #4; Back of figure — thermometer money meter
GRADE: E

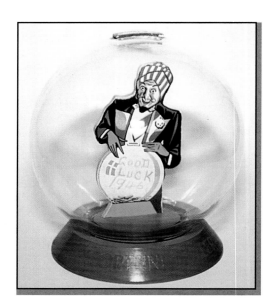

No.: BB-26
NAME: Swami, the Fortune Teller
HEIGHT: 6½"
SLOT: raised slot
INFO: Bottom label — see variation #2; Back of figure — thermometer money meter
GRADE: Very Rare

No.: BB-27
NAME: Stop Monkeying and Start Saving
HEIGHT: 6½"
SLOT: raised slot
INFO: monkey wearing long sleeves; Bottom label — see variation #4; Back of figure — thermometer money meter
GRADE: E

NO.: BB-28
NAME: King of the Jingle Lion
HEIGHT: 6½"
SLOT: raised slot
INFO: Bottom label — see variation #4; Back of figure — thermometer money meter
GRADE: E

See page 7 for price ranges.

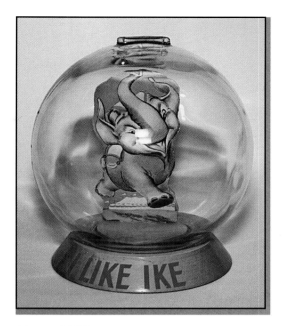

NO.: BB-29
NAME: I Like Ike Elephant
HEIGHT: 6½"
SLOT: raised slot
INFO: Bottom label — see variation #5; Back of figure — thermometer money meter
GRADE: Rare

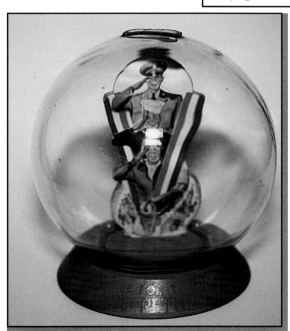

NO.: BB-30
NAME: Save for the Day He Returns
HEIGHT: 6½"
SLOT: raised slot
INFO: three servicemen; Bottom label — see variation #2; Back of figure — thermometer money meter
GRADE: F

NO.: BB-31
NAME: Change for the Baby
HEIGHT: 6½"
SLOT: raised slot
INFO: baby reaching out; Bottom label — see variation #5; Back of figure — thermometer money meter
GRADE: E

No.: BB-32
Name: Save for the New Baby
Height: 6½"
Slot: raised slot
Info: baby with rattle and beads; Bottom label — see variation #5; Back of figure — thermometer money meter
Grade: D

	PHOTO NOT AVAILABLE
No.:	BB-33
Name:	Save for Columbian Missions
Height:	6½"
Slot:	raised slot
Info:	Chinese boy with sign
Grade:	Rare

	PHOTO NOT AVAILABLE
No.:	BB-34
Name:	Money in the Bank
Height:	6½"
Slot:	raised slot
Info:	Schoeneman – For Fall, dollar bill on end
Grade:	Rare

Reported to Exist – Not Yet Found

Girl with Umbrella
A Penny a Drill Fits the Bill
Save for Vacation
Save for War Bonds
Save for the Tax Man
Save for Summer Fun
Save for Christmas
Save for College

RATING/GRADING	
A	To $15.00
B	$15.00 – 35.00
C	$35.00 – 75.00
D	$75.00 – 150.00
E	$150.00 – 300.00
F	$300.00 – 600.00
Rare	$600.00 – 1,000.00
Very Rare	negotiable

Bubble Bank Bottom Labels

1. The Bubble Bank "See Your Savings Swell" printed like glass bubble picture

2. The Bubble Bank "See Your Savings Swell" printed like glass bubble picture

3. The Bubble Bank "See Your Savings Swell" three red dots

4. The Bubble Bank "See Your Savings Swell" picture of three bubble banks

5. The Bubble Bank "See Your Savings Swell" picture of ten Bubble Banks; others may exist

Fish Bowl Banks

NO.: FB-1
NAME: Treasure Bowl
HEIGHT: 5"
SLOT: punched in lid
INFO: fish looking at coin; decal label on both sides; one-piece lid and lock; Pat. Pend., Bower Mfg. Co., Goshen, Ind.
GRADE: C

NO.: FB-2
NAME: Saving for a Vacation
Height: 5"
SLOT: punched in lid
INFO: black silhouettes; decal label on both sides; two-piece lid and lock; Pat. Pend., Bower Mfg. Co., Goshen, Ind.
GRADE: D

NO.: FB-3
NAME: Change for the Baby
HEIGHT: 5"
SLOT: punched in lid
INFO: baby and teddy bear; decal label on both sides; two-piece lid and lock; Pat. Pend., Bower Mfg. Co., Goshen, Ind.
GRADE: D

NO.: FB-4
NAME: Save for a New Car
HEIGHT: 5"
SLOT: punched in lid
INFO: car and billboard; decal label on both sides; one-piece lid and lock; Pat. Pend., Bower Mfg. Co., Goshen, Ind.
GRADE: D

NO.: FB-5
NAME: Treasure Bowl
HEIGHT: 5"
SLOT: punched in lid
INFO: fish looking at coin; decal label on both sides; two-piece lid and lock; Pat. Pend., Bower Mfg. Co., Goshen, Ind.
GRADE: C

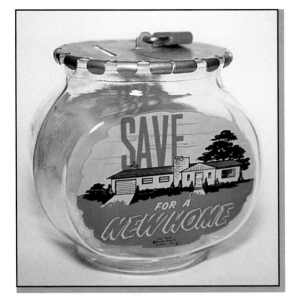

NO.: FB-6
NAME: Save for a New Home
HEIGHT: 5"
SLOT: punched in lid
INFO: Rambler house; decal label on both sides; two-piece lid and lock; Pat. Pend., Bower Mfg. Co., Goshen, Ind.
GRADE: D

NO.: FB-7
NAME: We Are Expecting
HEIGHT: 5"
SLOT: punched in lid
INFO: stork with checklist; decal label on both sides; one-piece lid and lock; Pat. Pend., Bower Mfg. Co., Goshen, Ind.
GRADE: E

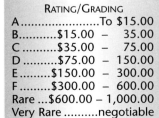

RATING/GRADING	
A	To $15.00
B	$15.00 – 35.00
C	$35.00 – 75.00
D	$75.00 – 150.00
E	$150.00 – 300.00
F	$300.00 – 600.00
Rare	$600.00 – 1,000.00
Very Rare	negotiable

NO.: FB-8
NAME: A Penny Saved Is a Penny Earned
HEIGHT: 5"
SLOT: punched in lid
INFO: colonial man with coin purse; decal label on both sides; one-piece lid and lock; Pat. Pend., Bower Mfg. Co., Goshen, Ind.
GRADE: E

NO.: FB-9
NAME: I'm a Tightwad
HEIGHT: 5"
SLOT: punched in lid
INFO: man on money pile; decal label on both sides; one-piece lid and lock; Pat. Pend., Bower Mfg. Co., Goshen, Ind.
GRADE: E

NO.: FB-10
NAME: Baby Change
HEIGHT: 5"
SLOT: punched in lid
INFO: baby wearing diaper; paper label on both sides; one-piece lid and lock; Pat. Pend., Bower Mfg. Co., Goshen, Ind.
GRADE: E

NO.: FB-11
NAME: Saving for my Church
HEIGHT: 5"
SLOT: punched in lid
INFO: paper label on both sides; one-piece lid and lock; Pat. Pend., Bower Mfg. Co., Goshen, Ind.
GRADE: F

NO.: FB-12
NAME: Feed the Kitty
HEIGHT: 5"
SLOT: punched in lid
INFO: tiger; paper label on both sides; one-piece lid and lock; Pat. Pend., Bower Mfg. Co., Goshen, Ind.
GRADE: E

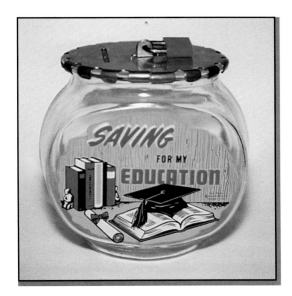

NO.: FB-13
NAME: Saving for my Education
HEIGHT: 5"
SLOT: punched in lid
INFO: books, diploma, and mortarboard; decal label on both sides; two-piece lid and lock; Pat. Pend., Bower Mfg. Co., Goshen, Ind.
GRADE: D

NO.: FB-14
NAME: Change Saver
HEIGHT: 5"
SLOT: punched in lid
INFO: baby wearing Scottish outfit; paper label on both sides; one-piece lid and lock; Pat. Pend., Bower Mfg. Co., Goshen, Ind.
GRADE: E

NO.: FB-15
NAME: Lots of Bucks
HEIGHT: 5"
SLOT: punched in lid
INFO: rider on bronco; paper label on both sides; one-piece lid and lock; Pat. Pend., Bower Mfg. Co., Goshen, Ind.
GRADE: E

NO.: FB-16
NAME: Shooting for Savings
HEIGHT: 5"
SLOT: punched in lid
INFO: rocket to moon; paper label on both sides; one-piece lid and lock; Pat. Pend., Bower Mfg. Co., Goshen, Ind.
GRADE: F

NO.: FB-17
NAME: Saving for My Blue Lodge
HEIGHT: 5"
SLOT: punched in lid
INFO: paper label on both sides; one-piece lid and lock; Pat. Pend., Bower Mfg. Co., Goshen, Ind.
GRADE: E

NO.: FB-18
NAME: Saving for My Scottish Rite
HEIGHT: 5"
SLOT: punched in lid
INFO: paper label on both sides; one-piece lid and lock; Pat. Pend., Bower Mfg. Co., Goshen, Ind.
Grade: E

NO.: FB-19
NAME: Reeves Banking and Trust Co., Dover, Ohio
HEIGHT: 5"
SLOT: punched in lid
INFO: Paper label — Reeves Bank; Decal label — Saving for a New Home; two-piece lid and lock; Pat. Pend., Bower Mfg. Co., Goshen, Ind.
GRADE: D

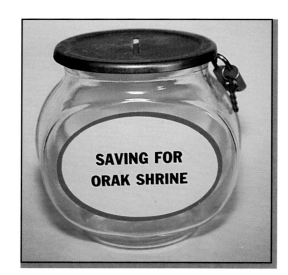

NO.: FB-20
NAME: Saving for Orak Shrine
HEIGHT: 5"
SLOT: punched in lid
INFO: paper label on both sides; one-piece lid and lock; Pat. Pend., Bower Mfg. Co., Goshen, Ind.
GRADE: E

NO.: FB-21
NAME: The Peoples Bank Co., Fort Recovery, Ohio
HEIGHT: 5"
SLOT: punched in lid
INFO: Decal label — Peoples Bank Co.; Decal label — We Are Expecting; one-piece lid and lock; Pat. Pend., Bower Mfg. Co. Goshen, Ind.
GRADE: E

NO.: FB-22
NAME: Treasure Bowl
HEIGHT: 5"
SLOT: punched in lid
INFO: pirate, fish, and treasure; paper label on both sides; one-piece lid and lock; Pat. Pend., Bower Mfg. Co., Goshen, Ind.
GRADE: E

NO.: FB-23
NAME: Pin Money
HEIGHT: 5"
SLOT: punched in lid
INFO: bowling ball striking pins; paper label on both sides; one-piece lid and lock; Pat. Pend., Bower Mfg. Co., Goshen, Ind.
GRADE: E

NO.: FB-24
NAME: Berwick Bank, Berwick, Penna.
HEIGHT: 5"
SLOT: punched in lid
INFO: Paper label — Berwick Bank; Decal label — Treasure Bowl; one-piece lid and lock; Pat. Pend., Bower Mfg. Co., Goshen, Ind.
GRADE: D

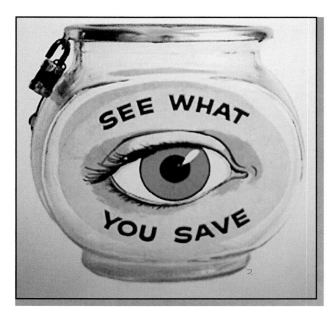

NO.: FB-25
NAME: See What You Save
HEIGHT: 5"
SLOT: punched in lid
INFO: large eye; paper label on both sides; one-piece lid and lock
GRADE: E

Glass Block Banks

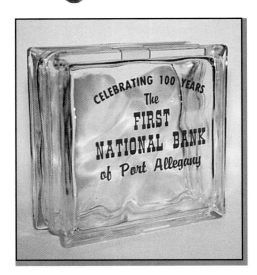

NO.: BL-1
NAME: First National Bank of Port Allegany, 100 Years Bank
HEIGHT: 7¾"
SLOT: molded in seam on top
INFO: decal label on front
GRADE: C

NO.: BL-2
NAME: Baseball Player
HEIGHT: 5¾"
SLOT: molded in seam on top
INFO: Bell Plastics, etched label
GRADE: C

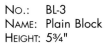

RATING/GRADING	
A	To $15.00
B	$15.00 – 35.00
C	$35.00 – 75.00
D	$75.00 – 150.00
E	$150.00 – 300.00
F	$300.00 – 600.00
Rare	$600.00 – 1,000.00
Very Rare	negotiable

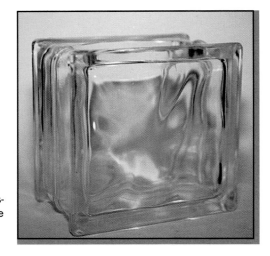

NO.: BL-3
NAME: Plain Block
HEIGHT: 5¾"
SLOT: large oval
INFO: clear with distorted pattern; change holder or vase
GRADE: B

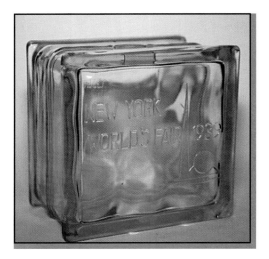

NO.: BL-4
NAME: 1939 New York World's Fair
HEIGHT: 5¾"
SLOT: molded in seam on top
INFO: Watch Your Savings Grow with Esso; raised lettering
GRADE: D

NO.: BL-5
NAME: Plain Block
HEIGHT: 5¾"
SLOT: molded in seam on top
INFO: clear with distorted pattern
GRADE: B

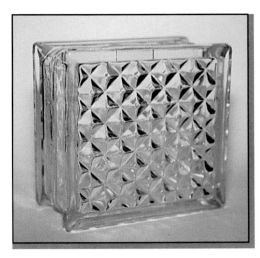

NO.:   BL-6
NAME: Diamond Pattern
HEIGHT: 5¾"
SLOT: molded in seam on top
INFO: pattern on inside of glass
GRADE: C

NO.:   BL-7
NAME: Glass Blower
Height: 4¾"
SLOT: molded in seam on top
INFO: label screened on glass; Corning Glass Works
GRADE: C

NO.:   BL-8
NAME: SoHio
HEIGHT: 4¾"
SLOT: molded in seam on top
INFO: See Your Savings, Enjoy Your Savings; Now You Can Watch Your Savings Grow, money amounts shown on chart; raised outside lettering
GRADE: D

NO.:   BL-9
NAME: Esso
HEIGHT: 4¾"
SLOT: molded in seam on top
INFO: Watch Your Savings Grow with Esso; Paper label — Save with your Esso bank to buy U. S. Defense Bonds; raised outside lettering
GRADE: D

NO.:   BL-10
NAME: Phillips 66
HEIGHT: 4¾"
SLOT: molded in seam on top
INFO: Phill-Up With Phillips 66; See What you Save; same on both sides with raised outside lettering
GRADE: D

NO.:   BL-11
NAME: People's Drug Stores, Inc.
Height: 4¾"
SLOT: molded in seam on top
INFO: See Your Savings, Shop Daily, People's Drug Stores Inc.; same on both sides with raised inside lettering
GRADE: C

NO.:   BL-12
NAME: Pittsburgh Paints
HEIGHT: 4¾"
SLOT: molded in seam on top
INFO: See Your Savings, picture of coins, Pittsburgh Paints; same on both sides with raised inside lettering
GRADE: D

NO.:   BL-13
NAME: Esso
HEIGHT: 4¾"
SLOT: molded in seam on top
INFO: Watch Your Savings Grow with Esso; same on both sides with raised outside lettering
GRADE: C

NO.:   BL-14
NAME: Scotsman
HEIGHT: 4¾"
SLOT: molded in seam on top
INFO: See Your Savings; same on both sides with raised inside lettering
GRADE: C

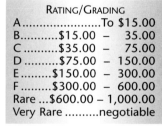

RATING/GRADING	
A	To $15.00
B	$15.00 – 35.00
C	$35.00 – 75.00
D	$75.00 – 150.00
E	$150.00 – 300.00
F	$300.00 – 600.00
Rare	$600.00 – 1,000.00
Very Rare	negotiable

NO.:   BL-15
NAME: Corning Glass Center
HEIGHT: 3¼"
SLOT: molded in seam on top
INFO: screened front label in blue; See Your Savings; same on both sides with raised inside lettering
GRADE: C

NO.:   BL-16
NAME: Foamglas Insulation
HEIGHT: 3¼"
SLOT: molded in seam on top
INFO: Save with Foamglas Insulation, large PC in right corner; same on both sides with raised inside lettering
GRADE: D

NO.: BL-17
NAME: Corning Foamglas Insulation
HEIGHT: 3¼"
SLOT: molded in seam on top
INFO: Save with Pittsburgh Corning Foamglas Insulation, PC in center rectangle; same on both sides with raised inside lettering
GRADE: D

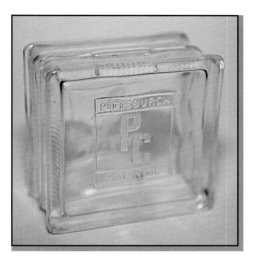

NO.: BL-18
NAME: Pittsburgh PC Corning
HEIGHT: 3¼"
SLOT: molded in seam on top
INFO: Pittsburgh, PC, Corning (in large square); same on both sides with raised inside lettering
GRADE: D

NO.: BL-19
NAME: 1940 New York World's Fair Glass Center
HEIGHT: 3¼"
SLOT: molded in seam on top
INFO: picture of Trilon and Perisphere; Back — Glass Center building; raised outside lettering
GRADE: D

NO.: BL-21
NAME: See Your Savings
HEIGHT: 3¼"
SLOT: molded in seam on top
INFO: See Your Savings on front, inside lettering; Back — plain glass with green paper label To Break Label
GRADE: C

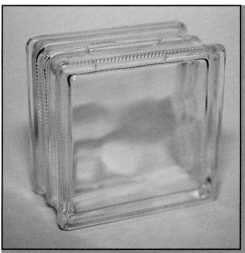

NO.: BL-20
NAME: Plain Block
HEIGHT: 3¼"
SLOT: molded in seam on top
INFO: plain with slightly distorted pattern
GRADE: B

No.: BL-22
NAME: United Glass Workers Local 53, Charleroi, Pa.
HEIGHT: 3¼"
SLOT: molded in seam on top
INFO: frosted glass on both sides, screened label on both sides; Back — Mortgage Burning, April 22, 1963
GRADE: D

No.: BL-24
NAME: Golden Gate International Exposition, 1940
HEIGHT: 3¼"
SLOT: molded in seam on top
INFO: Back — Treasure Island On San Francisco Bay, Fair in '40; in raised outside lettering
GRADE: D

No.: BL-23
NAME: Chicago 1954 A.F.G.W.U., Local 1004 PC
HEIGHT: 3¼"
SLOT: molded in seam on top
INFO: paper label
GRADE: D

No.: BL-25
NAME: Pittsburgh Paints Sun Face
HEIGHT: 3¼"
SLOT: molded in seam on top
INFO: raised outside lettering Save with Pittsburgh Paints, Smooth as Glass; smiling sun face on back
GRADE: D

No.: BL-26
NAME: 1776, Happy Birthday U.S.A., Port Allgany, Pennsylvania, 1976
HEIGHT: 3¼"
SLOT: molded in seam on top
INFO: large Liberty Bell with pebble grain finish around it; same on both sides with raised inside lettering
GRADE: D

No.:   BL-27
Name: Bank On Ike
Height: 3¼"
Slot: molded in seam on top
Info: screened on label in dark green, President Ike on elephant; Bottom — oval trap opening that had paper glued on
Grade: E

RATING/GRADING	
A	To $15.00
B	$15.00 – 35.00
C	$35.00 – 75.00
D	$75.00 – 150.00
E	$150.00 – 300.00
F	$300.00 – 600.00
Rare	$600.00 – 1,000.00
Very Rare	negotiable

No.:   BL-28
Name: Plain Change Holder
Height: 3¼"
Slot: large oval
Info: plain with slightly distorted pattern
Grade: B

No.:   BL-29
Name: Watch Your Savings Grow With Standard Oil Products
Height: 4¾"
Slot: molded in seam on top
Info: same on both sides with raised lettering
Grade: D

No.:   BL-30
Name: Liberty Lodge 505, 1873 – 1973
Height: 3¼"
Slot: molded in seam on top
Info: screened label on front; Masonic Emblem; same on both sides with raised lettering
Grade: D

No.:   BL-31
Name: 1982 World's Fair, Knoxville, Tenn.
Height: 5¾"
Slot: molded in seam on top
Info: screened front label
Grade: D

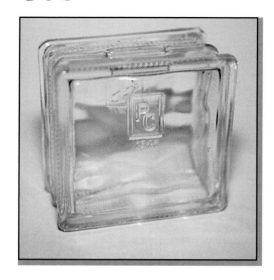

No.: BL-32
Name: PC 1947
Height: 3¼"
Slot: molded in seam on top
Info: PC in rectangle with 1947 below; same on both sides with raised inside lettering
Grade: D

No.: BL-33
Name: Kokopelli
Height: 5¾"
Slot: molded in seam on top
Info: Kokopelli figure etched in front; Jerome, New Mexico
Grade: D

No.: BL-34
Name: Diamondback Gecko
Height: 5¾"
Slot: molded in seam on top
Info: diamondback gecko etched on front of bank; Jerome, New Mexico
Grade: D

No.: BL-36
Name: Southwest Church
Height: 5¾"
Slot: molded in seam on top
Info: Southwest Church with five crosses etched in layers on front; Jerome, New Mexico
Grade: D

No.: BL-35
Name: Bear
Height: 5¾"
Slot: molded in seam on top
Info: bear with lightning arrow etched on front of bank; Jerome, New Mexico
Grade: D

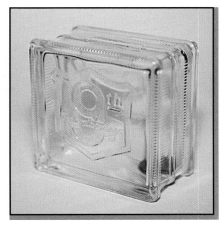

No.:   BL-37
NAME: SBCC Rocking Horse
HEIGHT: 5¾"
SLOT: molded in seam on top
INFO: SBCC Rocking Horse Bank etched on front of bank; 1989 Convention, Buffalo, N.Y.; only 12 made
GRADE: D

No.:   BL-38
NAME: Rotary International
HEIGHT: 3¼"
SLOT: molded in seam on top
INFO: decal label on front
GRADE: D

No.:   BL-39
NAME: 9th Federal Savings
HEIGHT: 3¼"
SLOT: molded in seam on top
INFO: same on both sides with raised inside lettering
GRADE: D

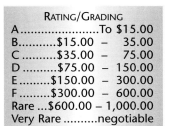

RATING/GRADING	
A	To $15.00
B	$15.00 – 35.00
C	$35.00 – 75.00
D	$75.00 – 150.00
E	$150.00 – 300.00
F	$300.00 – 600.00
Rare	$600.00 – 1,000.00
Very Rare	negotiable

No.:   BL-40
NAME: American Revolution Bicenten-
        nial Bank, 1776 – 1976
HEIGHT: 3¼"
SLOT: molded in seam on top
INFO: paper label on front
GRADE: D

No.:   BL-41
NAME: Save For Christ Mother &
        Daughter Banquet
HEIGHT: 3¼"
SLOT: molded in seam on top
INFO: screened label on front
GRADE: D

No.:   BL-42
NAME: St. Louis, Missouri, Mason
        Contractors, February 18 –
        21, 1967
HEIGHT: 3¼"
SLOT: molded in seam on top
INFO: decal label on front
GRADE: D

NO.: BL-43
NAME: Quality Service Standard with Chevrons
HEIGHT: 4¾"
SLOT: molded in seam on top
INFO: Back — Save with Standard, raised outside lettering; Paper label — Buy War Bonds
GRADE: E

NO.: BL-44
NAME: 1939 New York World's Fair
HEIGHT: 4¾"
SLOT: molded in seam on top
INFO: Paper label — War Bonds; picture of Trilon and Perisphere; Back — Watch Your Savings Grow with Esso
GRADE: E

NO.: BL-45
NAME: Watch Your Savings Grow with Esso
HEIGHT: 4¾"
SLOT: molded in seam on top
INFO: non-war label; same on both sides with raised outside lettering; Paper label — Save for Christmas, vacation, new car, clothing
GRADE: E

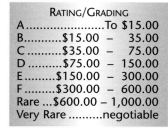

RATING/GRADING	
A	To $15.00
B	$15.00 – 35.00
C	$35.00 – 75.00
D	$75.00 – 150.00
E	$150.00 – 300.00
F	$300.00 – 600.00
Rare	$600.00 – 1,000.00
Very Rare	negotiable

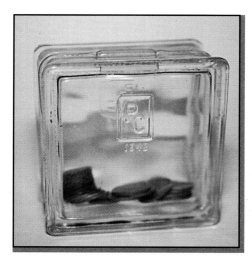

NO.: BL-46
NAME: PC 1948
HEIGHT: 3¼"
SLOT: molded in seam on top
INFO: PC in rectangle with 1948 below; same on both sides with raised inside lettering
GRADE: D

NO.: BL-47
NAME: SBCCA 31st Convention
HEIGHT: 5¾"
SLOT: molded in seam on top
INFO: etched design in front
GRADE: D

No.: BL-48
NAME: Corning Glass Center
HEIGHT: 3¼"
SLOT: molded in seam on top
INFO: screened front label in white; See Your Savings on both sides with raised inside lettering
GRADE: C

No.: BL-49
NAME: Largest Block
HEIGHT: 11¾"
SLOT: molded in seam on top
INFO: very clear glass; PCC Metro Dade, raised outside letters molded in reverse, on top and bottom
GRADE: C

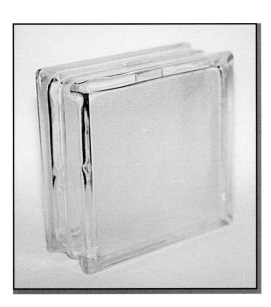

No.: BL-50
NAME: Crystal Grain Pattern Block
HEIGHT: 7¾"
SLOT: molded in seam on top
INFO: crystal clear glass with grain pattern molded on inside on both sides
GRADE: C

No.: BL-51
NAME: Two-sided Corner Block
HEIGHT: 7¾"
SLOT: molded in seam on top
INFO: very clear glass on large flat sides, distorted pattern on two front edges
GRADE: D

No.: BL-52
NAME: Round Front Edge Block
HEIGHT: 7¾"
SLOT: molded in seam on top
INFO: clear with distorted pattern
GRADE: D

No.: BL-54
NAME: Flint Glass Workers Union
HEIGHT: 3¼"
SLOT: molded in seam on top
INFO: decal label on front
GRADE: D

No.: BL-53
NAME: Vertical Rectangular Block
HEIGHT: 7¾"
SLOT: molded in seam on top
INFO: very clear glass front and back; PCC Metro Dade, molded in one side in raised outside letters in reverse
GRADE: C

No.: BL-55
NAME: Corning Glass Works, A.F.G.W.U. of North America
HEIGHT: 4¾"
SLOT: molded in seam on top
INFO: decal label on front
GRADE: D

No.: BL-56
NAME: Six-Sided Block
HEIGHT: 7¾"
SLOT: molded in seam on top
INFO: very clear glass on all sides
GRADE: D

No.: BL-57
NAME: Football Player, Bell Plastics
HEIGHT: 5¾"
SLOT: molded in seam on top
INFO: etched front label
GRADE: C

NO.: BL-58
NAME: Round Top Block
HEIGHT: 7¾"
SLOT: molded in seam on top
INFO: clear sides with slightly distorted pattern
GRADE: D

NO.: BL-59
NAME: Dei Viget Sub Numine
HEIGHT: 3¼"
SLOT: molded in seam on top
INFO: decal label on front; See Your Savings, raised inside letters on both sides
GRADE: D

NO.: BL-60
NAME: Masonic Emblem
HEIGHT: 3¼"
SLOT: molded in seam on top
INFO: emblem molded, raised on the inside
GRADE: D

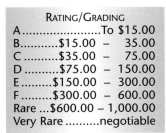

RATING/GRADING	
A	To $15.00
B	$15.00 – 35.00
C	$35.00 – 75.00
D	$75.00 – 150.00
E	$150.00 – 300.00
F	$300.00 – 600.00
Rare	$600.00 – 1,000.00
Very Rare	negotiable

NO.: BL-61
NAME: Original 200 in Disc Corning Glass Center, N.Y.
HEIGHT: 3¼"
SLOT: molded in seam on top
INFO: screened label in blue on front; See Your Savings on the back in raised inside lettering
GRADE: D

NO.: BL-62
NAME: Betty Boop
HEIGHT: 5¾"
SLOT: molded in seam on top
INFO: etched Betty Boop on both sides
GRADE: D

No.: BL-63
NAME: Pyrex Laboratory Glass Ware
HEIGHT: 3¼"
SLOT: molded in seam on top
INFO: screened label on front in green; Saves You Money
GRADE: D

No.: BL-64
NAME: Watchman Retreat, August, 1977
HEIGHT: 3¼"
SLOT: molded in seam on top
INFO: screened front label in black; Deeper In Him
GRADE: D

No.: BL-65
NAME: Iowa Fiber Box
HEIGHT: 3¼"
SLOT: molded in seam on top
INFO: paper label on front
GRADE: D

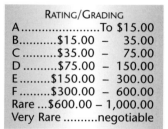

RATING/GRADING	
A	To $15.00
B	$15.00 – 35.00
C	$35.00 – 75.00
D	$75.00 – 150.00
E	$150.00 – 300.00
F	$300.00 – 600.00
Rare	$600.00 – 1,000.00
Very Rare	negotiable

No.: BL-66
NAME: Gardner-Denver
HEIGHT: 5¾"
SLOT: molded in seam on top
INFO: etched label on front
GRADE: D

No.: BL-67
NAME: William J. Hart, United Steel Workers
HEIGHT: 3¼"
SLOT: molded in seam on top
INFO: front paper label with names screened in blue
GRADE: D

No.: BL-68
NAME: Wizard of Oz
HEIGHT: 3¼"
SLOT: molded in seam on top
INFO: Wizard of Oz characters in raised outside image on front of bank; Loew's, Inc.
GRADE: E

No.: BL-69
Name: Holy Family League of Charity
Height: 4¾"
Slot: molded in seam on top
Info: molded scene of woman and child knocking at a door within a large heart; molded on the inside on both sides
Grade: D

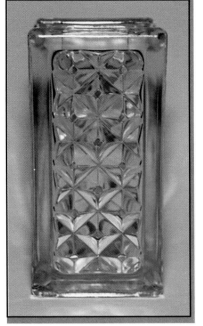

No.: BL-70
Name: Tall Rectangular Block
Height: 7¾"
Slot: molded in seam on top
Info: diamond pattern molded inside glass on both sides
Grade: C

No.: BL-71
Name: M.C.A.A. Show Atlanta, PC 73
Height: 3¼"
Slot: molded in seam on top
Info: label screened on front in blue
Grade: D

No.: BL-72
Name: Shop and Save at Thrift Drug Stores
Height: 3¼"
Slot: molded in seam on top
Info: image molded on inside of both sides
Grade: D

No.: BL-73
Name: Santa Corning Christmas Party 1962
Height: 3¼"
Slot: molded in seam on top
Info: etched glass on front and back; Front — Santa screened in red; Back — screened in green
Grade: E

NO.: BL-74
NAME: Santa Fe Logo
HEIGHT: 4½"
SLOT: molded in plastic top trap
INFO: Front — etched Santa Fe logo;
Bottom — Made in Germany in raised outside letters
GRADE: C

NO.: BL-75
NAME: Ohringer's Your Friendly Furniture Store
HEIGHT: 4¾"
SLOT: molded in seam on top
INFO: molded on inside of both sides;
Braddock, McKeesport, and Greensburg
GRADE: E

NO.: BL-76
NAME: Save For Liberty
HEIGHT: 3¼"
SLOT: molded in seam on top
INFO: full paper label on front
GRADE: E

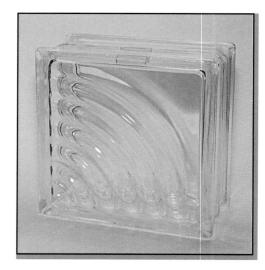

NO.: BL-77
NAME: Arc Line
HEIGHT: 7¾"
SLOT: molded in seam on top
INFO: clear glass block with concentric arc lines radiating from the lower left corner; molded on the inside of both sides
GRADE: C

NO.: BL-78
NAME: Dr. Pepper
HEIGHT: 4½"
SLOT: molded in seam on top
INFO: Dr. Pepper logo etched on front; rectangular plastic trap in bottom; Made in Germany in raised outside letters top and bottom
GRADE: C

NO.: BL-79
NAME: Harley-Davidson
Motorcycles
HEIGHT: 4½"
SLOT: molded in seam on top
INFO: Harley-Davidson logo etched on front; rectangular plastic trap in bottom; Made in Germany in raised outside letters top and bottom
GRADE: C

NO.: BL-80
NAME: E.C. Simmons Keen Kutter
HEIGHT: 4½"
SLOT: molded in seam on top
INFO: E.C. Simmons Keen Kutter logo etched on front; rectangular plastic trap in bottom; Made in Germany in raised outside letters top and bottom
GRADE: C

NO.: BL-81
NAME: You Always Save at Cunningham's Drug Stores
HEIGHT: 3¼"
SLOT: molded in seam on top
INFO: clear glass block with raised outside lettering; Back — See Your Savings
GRADE: D

NO.: BL-82
NAME: New York Central System Logo
HEIGHT: 4½"
SLOT: molded in plastic top trap
INFO: New York Central system logo etched on front; Made in Germany in raised outside letters top and bottom
GRADE: C

NO.: BL-83
NAME: Locust Glass Inc.
HEIGHT: 3¼"
SLOT: molded in seam on top
INFO: Full paper label on front — St. Louis', Oldest Auto Glass Service; Back — Save with Pittsburgh Corning Glass Blocks; raised lettering molded inside
GRADE: D

No.: BL-84
NAME: Save with Standard, Buy War Savings Bonds
HEIGHT: 4¾"
SLOT: molded in seam on top
INFO: clear glass block with raised outside lettering; Back — Quality Service, Standard, two chevrons
GRADE: E

No.: BL-85
NAME: Old Friends Are Worth Keeping
HEIGHT: 4¾"
SLOT: molded in seam on top
INFO: paper label on front
GRADE: D

No.: BL-86
NAME: The First National Bank, Port Allegany, 100 Years, 1988
HEIGHT: 7¾"
SLOT: molded in seam on top
INFO: clear plastic front label
GRADE: D

No.: BL-87
NAME: Save with H.L. Bennett
HEIGHT: 4¾"
SLOT: molded in seam on top
INFO: label screened on front in blue
GRADE: D

No.: BL-88
NAME: Watchman Retreat
"God, Country and
You," 1966
HEIGHT: 3¼"
SLOT: molded in seam on
top
INFO: label screened on
front in black
GRADE: D

No.: BL-89
NAME: Ohio Flower and State
HEIGHT: 5¾"
SLOT: molded in seam on top
INFO: label screened on front in red
GRADE: D

RATING/GRADING	
A	To $15.00
B	$15.00 – 35.00
C	$35.00 – 75.00
D	$75.00 – 150.00
E	$150.00 – 300.00
F	$300.00 – 600.00
Rare	$600.00 – 1,000.00
Very Rare	negotiable

No.: BL-90
NAME: Jamestown Teacher's Federal
Credit Union, 1940 – 1965
HEIGHT: 3¼"
SLOT: molded in seam on top
INFO: paper label on front
GRADE: D

No.: BL-91
NAME: Americorps National Service
HEIGHT: 5¾"
SLOT: molded in seam on top
INFO: label etched on front
GRADE: D

No.: BL-92
NAME: Mirror Block
HEIGHT: 7¾"
SLOT: molded in seam on top
INFO: gold mirror surface on front
GRADE: D

NO.: BL-93
NAME: Northern Pacific Railway
HEIGHT: 4½"
SLOT: molded in plastic top trap
INFO: logo label etched on front; Bottom — Made in Germany, raised outside letters
GRADE: C

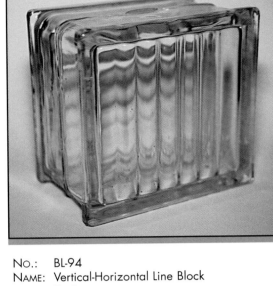

NO.: BL-94
NAME: Vertical-Horizontal Line Block
HEIGHT: 7¾"
SLOT: molded in seam on top
INFO: clear glass with vertical lines molded on front; horizontal lines molded on the back; both sides are molded on the inside
GRADE: C

NO.: BL-95
NAME: Pittsburgh Paints
HEIGHT: 3¼"
SLOT: molded in seam on top
INFO: Save With Pittsburgh Paints, Smooth as Glass raised outside lettering; Back — smiling sun face; Paper label — opening inst. adv. wallhide, sun-proof, florhide and waterspar paints
GRADE: E

NO.: BL-96
NAME: Ohio State Buckeye
HEIGHT: 5¾"
SLOT: molded in seam on top
INFO: label screened on front in red
GRADE: C

NO.: BL-97
NAME: Union Pacific
HEIGHT: 4½"
SLOT: molded in plastic top trap
INFO: logo etched on front; Bottom — Made in Germany, raised outside lettering
GRADE: C

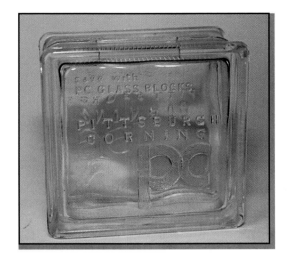

NO.: BL-98
NAME: PC Glass
HEIGHT: 3¼"
SLOT: molded in seam on top
INFO: Save with PC Glass blocks at top, Pittsburgh Corning in middle, PC logo at bottom right, raised inside letters
GRADE: C

NO.: BL-99
NAME: Save with Glass
HEIGHT: 3¼"
SLOT: molded in seam on top
INFO: Save With Corning box logo in middle, glass blocks, raised inside letters
GRADE: C

RATING/GRADING	
A	To $15.00
B	$15.00 – 35.00
C	$35.00 – 75.00
D	$75.00 – 150.00
E	$150.00 – 300.00
F	$300.00 – 600.00
Rare	$600.00 – 1,000.00
Very Rare	negotiable

NO.: BL-100
NAME: Charter Member National Home Gardening Club
HEIGHT: 5¾"
SLOT: molded in seam on top
INFO: metallic label on front
GRADE: B

NO.: BL-101
NAME: Case XX
HEIGHT: 5¾"
SLOT: molded in seam on top
INFO: Case XX Knives logo on front; logo embossed on outside with grain finish on lettering and front edge of the block
GRADE: B

NO.: BL-102
NAME: Zippo
HEIGHT: 5¾"
SLOT: molded in seam on top
INFO: Zippo Lighters logo on front; logo embossed on outside with grain finish to background
GRADE: B

Advertising Mug Banks

NO.: AM-1
NAME: Fat Willy's Bar-B-Q Coca-Cola Logo
HEIGHT: 5¼"
SLOT: punched
INFO: screened in red on two sides; metal lid; most significant advertising mugs known; one of six used in the movie Primary Colors
GRADE: D

NO.: AM-2
NAME: Chantilly Vocational Career Center
HEIGHT: 4⅞"
SLOT: molded in lid
INFO: screened and pyro glazed in red; plastic lid
GRADE: A

NO.: AM-3
NAME: EMC Equity Mortgage Corp.
HEIGHT: 4⅞"
SLOT: molded in lid
INFO: screened in blue; plastic lid, Grand Opening, 1987, Heimburger Branch
GRADE: B

NO.: AM-4
NAME: Thanks! Doug Dodge, General Chairman, Central Maryland United Way
HEIGHT: 4⅞"
SLOT: molded in lid
INFO: screened in green and purple, plastic lid, We put the money to work
GRADE: B

NO.: AM-5
NAME: Midrin — You Can Bank on It!
HEIGHT: 4⅞"
SLOT: punched
INFO: screened in red on white; metal lid; Carnrick Laboratories, Inc.
GRADE: A

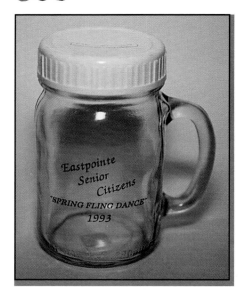

NO.: AM-6
NAME: Eastpointe Senior Citizens Spring Fling Dance, 1993
HEIGHT: 5⅜"
SLOT: punched in plastic lid
INFO: screened in purple
GRADE: A

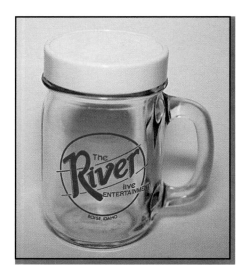

NO.: AM-7
NAME: The River, Live Entertainment, Boise, Idaho
HEIGHT: 5"
SLOT: molded in lid
INFO: screened in red; plastic lid
GRADE: A

NO.: AM-8
NAME: New York (Big Apple)
HEIGHT: 3⅜"
SLOT: molded in lid
INFO: screened and pyro glazed in black, red, and white; plastic lid; 1993, The Paradies Collection
GRADE: B

NO.: AM-9
NAME: Texas (Cactus)
HEIGHT: 3⅜"
SLOT: molded in lid
INFO: screened and pyro glazed in black and yellow; plastic lid; 1993, The Paradies Collection
GRADE: B

NO.: AM-10
NAME: Washington, D.C. (Capitol)
HEIGHT: 3⅜"
SLOT: molded in lid
INFO: screened and pyro glazed in blue, red, and white; plastic lid; 1993, The Paradies Collection
GRADE: B

NO.: AM-11
NAME: Don't Mess With Texas (Star)
HEIGHT: 3⅜"
SLOT: molded in lid
INFO: screened and pyro glazed in red, white, and blue; plastic lid; 1993, The Paradies Collection
GRADE: B

No.: AM-12
NAME: Watch Your Money Grow at First
National Bank, Mifflintown/Port
Royal
HEIGHT: 3⅜"
SLOT: molded in lid
INFO: screened in blue; plastic lid,
Bank On Us
GRADE: B

No.: AM-13
NAME: North American Beauty Services
HEIGHT: 4⅞"
SLOT: molded in lid
INFO: screened in maroon; plastic lid
GRADE: A

No.: AM-14
NAME: Delaware Volunteer Fireman's Associ-
ation, 61st Annual Convention
HEIGHT: 4⅞"
SLOT: punched
INFO: screened in gold and blue on white;
two-piece metal lid
GRADE: A

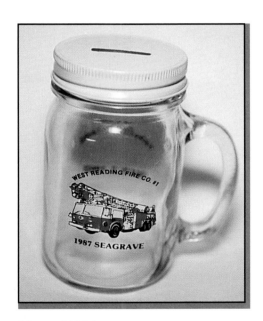

No.: AM-15
NAME: Westside "Walk In" Sinking Spring,
Pennsylvania
HEIGHT: 4⅞"
SLOT: molded in lid
INFO: screened in red; plastic lid
GRADE: A

No.: AM-16
NAME: West Reading Fire Co. #1, 1987,
Seagrave
HEIGHT: 4⅞"
SLOT: punched
INFO: screened in black, red, and white;
metal lid
GRADE: A

NO.: AM-17
NAME: Quakertown Flight Festival,
1983
HEIGHT: 4⅞"
SLOT: molded in lid
INFO: screened in blue on silver;
plastic lid
GRADE: A

NO.: AM-18
NAME: Ladies Auxiliary Ruscombmanor
Fire Co.
HEIGHT: 4⅞"
SLOT: punched
INFO: screened in red; metal lid
GRADE: A

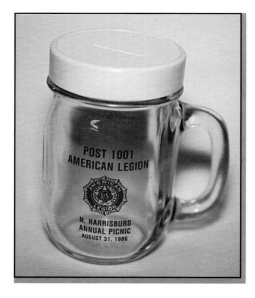

RATING/GRADING	
A ....To $15.00	
B ....$15.00 – 35.00	
C ....$35.00 – 75.00	
D ....$75.00 – 150.00	
E ....$150.00 – 300.00	
F ....$300.00 – 600.00	
Rare ...$600.00 – 1,000.00	
Very Rare ....negotiable	

NO.: AM-19
NAME: Post 1001 American Legion
HEIGHT: 4⅞"
SLOT: molded in lid
INFO: screened in blue; plastic lid
GRADE: A

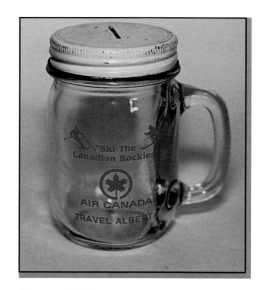

NO.: AM-20
NAME: Ski the Canadian Rockies, Air Canada
HEIGHT: 4⅞"
SLOT: punched
INFO: screened in red; metal lid
GRADE: A

NO.: AM-21
NAME: Upstairs Dinner Theater,
Omaha
HEIGHT: 4⅞"
SLOT: molded in lid
INFO: screened in blue; plastic lid
GRADE: A

NO.: AM-22
NAME: Grab Us, We're Great, Coast Line Travel
HEIGHT: 4⅞"
SLOT: punched
INFO: screened in blue; metal lid
GRADE: A

NO.: AM-23
NAME: Get a Grip on your Financial Future, Jonestown Bank & Trust Company
HEIGHT: 4⅞"
SLOT: punched
INFO: screened in black; metal lid
GRADE: A

NO.: AM-24
NAME: Central Trust & Savings Bank, Geneseo, Illinois
HEIGHT: 4⅞"
SLOT: punched
INFO: screened in black; metal lid
GRADE: A

NO.: AM-25
NAME: Nolamine, You Can Bank On It!
HEIGHT: 4⅞"
SLOT: punched
INFO: screened red on white; metal lid
GRADE: A

NO.: AM-26
NAME: 1st National Bank, Shreveport/ Bossier
HEIGHT: 3⅜"
SLOT: molded in lid
INFO: screened in black; plastic lid
GRADE: B

NO.: AM-27
NAME: Kids Across America
HEIGHT: 5¾"
SLOT: molded in lid
INFO: screened in silver gray; plastic lid
GRADE: B

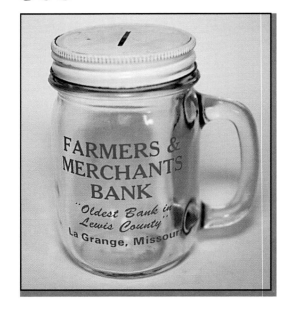

NO.: AM-28
NAME: Farmers & Merchants Bank, La Grange, Missouri
HEIGHT: 4⅞"
SLOT: punched
INFO: screened in green; metal lid
GRADE: A

NO.: AM-29
NAME: University of Maryland Terrapins
HEIGHT: 5¼"
SLOT: punched
INFO: screened in black on orange; metal lid
GRADE: A

RATING/GRADING	
A	To $15.00
B	$15.00 – 35.00
C	$35.00 – 75.00
D	$75.00 – 150.00
E	$150.00 – 300.00
F	$300.00 – 600.00
Rare	$600.00 – 1,000.00
Very Rare	negotiable

NO.: AM-30
NAME: I'm Pepsi – I'm Pete, Pepsi-Cola
HEIGHT: 5"
SLOT: molded in lid
INFO: screened in blue; fuzzy ball with eyes and Pepsi label ribbon; plastic lid
GRADE: B

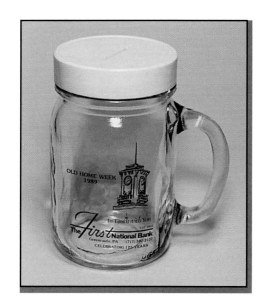

NO.: AM-31
NAME: Old Home Week, The First National Bank, Greencastle, PA, 1989
HEIGHT: 4⅞"
SLOT: molded in lid
INFO: screened in blue; plastic lid
GRADE: A

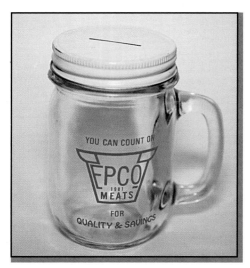

NO.: AM-32
NAME: You Can Count on PCO Meats, 1981
HEIGHT: 4⅞"
SLOT: punched
INFO: screened in red; metal lid
GRADE: A

No.:   AM-33
Name: First Federal Bank of Greene County
Height: 4⅞"
Slot: punched
Info: screened and pyro glazed in yellow, green, and black; metal lid; Save Systematically
Grade: A

No.:   AM-34
Name: Woodsboro Bank, 1899 – 1995
Height: 5⅜"
Slot: punched in plastic lid
Info: screened in green; plastic lid
Grade: A

No.:   AM-35
Name: Texas (four chili peppers)
Height: 3⅜"
Slot: molded in lid
Info: screened and pyro glazed red; plastic lid
Grade: B

No.:   AM-36
Name: Leesport Farmers Market, 1947 – 1997
Height: 5¼"
Slot: molded in lid
Info: screened and pyro glazed red and black; plastic lid
Grade: B

Folk Art Hand Painted

These were painted at home by their owners after using the contents.

Look-Alikes

These banks *look-alike* glass banks and are sometimes referred to as glass banks ...especially on the Internet.

Articles, Ads & Patents

TWO GLASS BANKS

Much is heard these days of some of the glass banks blown at Sandwich. Undeniably, these whimsies are superb examples of the glass blower's art, but equally certain it is that they are more representative of the blower than of any peculiarly national characteristic. Nor did Sandwich workmen alone produce these magnificent proofs of craftsmanship, as the bank was always a popular conceit with the glass blower.

The two pressed banks illustrated on this page are as American as Baseball, as typical of their era as the shaving mug. Today they are desirable additions to a collection of banks, and are equally desirable in a collection of glass. They are reproduced from a catalogue issued in 1887 by McKee and Brothers, Pittsburg, Pennsylvania. The Cabinet Bank at the right is 3¼″ high, and the Dome Bank is 4¼″ tall.

Cabinet Bank
FULL SIZE

No iron bank ever caught more deftly the feeling of a small village bank than does the one designated Cabinet, and no piece ever illustrated by the glassmakers, who were, at that time, systematically exploiting our yet young sense of nationalism, ever appealed more directly to the readily-aroused feeling of patriotism latent in the American heart, than does the Dome Bank. As though the stars which liberally adorn the dome, itself reminiscent of many of our public buildings, were insufficient reminders of the nationalistic character of this bank, the artist has contrived to show us coins bearing Liberty, the American Eagle, and the phrase, United States of America.

Pieces of this sort capture all the whimsy and nostalgia of a period forever passed, and serve, today, to remind us bluntly and with no subtlety, of the heritage which is, and can remain, ours.

Dome Bank Full Size

A GUIDE TO AMERICAN NURSING BOTTLES

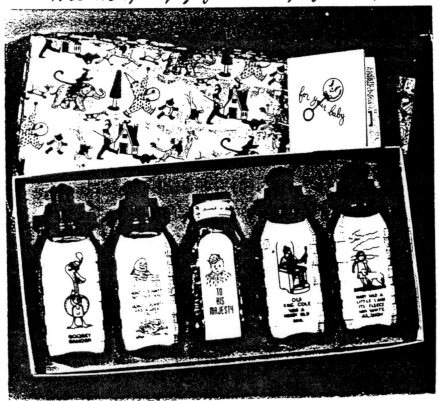

His Majesty Gift Package for Boys

WELCOME THE NEW ARRIVAL
With This Beautiful and Useful Gift

NEW WIDE MOUTH DECORATED NURSERS

Complete with Cap, Nipple, Disc assembly — with those Featured Nipples

RHYMES — DESIGNS — ASSORTED COLORS
Center Unit — NURSA BANK

DEFINITE PLAN READY TO OPERATE

YOUR FEATURED AD ON:

- LABEL ON INSIDE BOX LID
- GIFT CARD IN EACH PACKAGE
- AMPLE SUPPLY OF POSTAL CARDS

REGISTER BOOKS — FOR YOUR FUTURE LEAD LIST

Sample and Complete Data and Information, Without Obligation, Upon Request.

WRITE TO-DAY

A PRODUCT OF

SAMUEL CALLET COMPANY
6541 ROSEMOOR STREET • PITTSBURGH 17, PA.

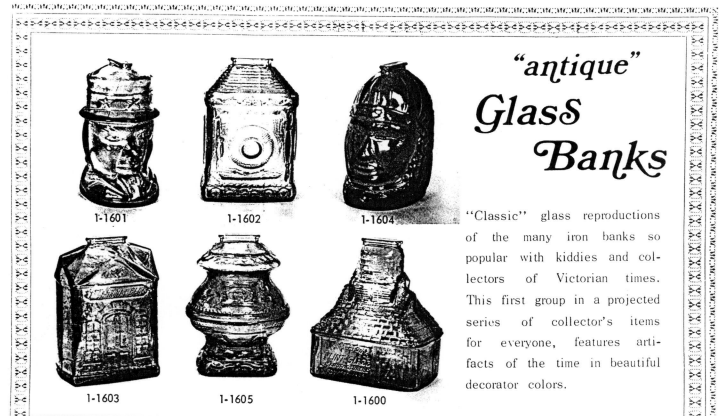

1-1601   1-1602   1-1604

1-1603   1-1605   1-1600

"antique" Glass Banks

"Classic" glass reproductions of the many iron banks so popular with kiddies and collectors of Victorian times. This first group in a projected series of collector's items for everyone, features artifacts of the time in beautiful decorator colors.

LIMITED EDITION

Early American

GLASS COIN BANK

SAVERS AT FIRST NATIONAL CAN GET A LIMITED EDITION EARLY AMERICAN GLASS COIN BANK COMMEMORATING THE BANK'S 150TH ANNIVERSARY. YOU CAN GET THE BANK FREE OR AT A REDUCED PRICE* WHEN YOU MAKE A QUALIFYING DEPOSIT TO A NEW OR EXISTING NOW ACCOUNT, PASSBOOK OR STATEMENT SAVINGS ACCOUNT.

HERE'S HOW IT WORKS

YOU DEPOSIT	BANK COST
$500	FREE
$300	$1.00
$150	$2.00
$100	$3.00

*ONE GIFT BANK PER ACCOUNT PLEASE. OFFER GOOD WHILE SUPPLY LASTS.

First National Trust Bank

Est. 1831

SUNBURY • MT. CARMEL • KULPMONT
SHAMOKIN DAM • BEAVERTOWN • OAKLYN

Member Federal Reserve Member F.D.I.C.

Liberty Bell Brand Jelly Bank
Trade Card

This circa 1885 trade card, is the only known trade card for a Glass Bank at this time. Only a few of these have been found. The trade card is for Liberty Bell Brand Jelly. It is printed in color on a medium weight paper and sized 2-3/4" x 4". The picture shows two little girls putting a coin in the Glass Bell Bank on a table, while a ship passes by with advertising for the jelly company on the sails. Four devilish monkeys are tolling a bell with the Robinson & Loeble trade name. The back of the card introduces the product to the public and gives a history of the real Liberty Bell, followed by instructions on removing the jelly from the glass container.

The Glass Bell Banks come in Clear, Amber, Blue and Milk Glass. The coin slot is on the top edge and has to be punched out of the glass. The bottom is a screw on tin lid with the name ROBINSON & LOEBLE / 723 WHARTON ST/ PHILA PA in embossed letters. Two different styles of scrolls and designs were used on the inside top of the bell to give the jelly a fancy look when it comes out of the glass.

LIBERTY BELL BRAND OF JELLY.

To THE PUBLIC AT LARGE:

We beg leave to introduce to your notice our "LIBERTY BELL" brand of JELLIES, also to say a few words about the same.

"This Bell is an exact copy in glass of the far-famed Liberty Bell of Philadelphia, which was cast in London, in the year 1751; arrived in Philadelphia, August, 1752; was again recast in 1753. Its weight is 2,080 pounds. July 8th, 1776, near the hour of twelve, the Bell was rung for the proclamation of the Declaration of Independence."

In September 1777, it was taken down and wagoned to Allentown, under an escort of Virginia and North Carolina troops, commanded by COL. POLK of North Carolina; returned to Philadelphia, June 18th, 1778, after the evacuation of the city.

On July 8th, 1835, the Bell was tolled for the last time at the funeral obsequies of JOHN MARSHALL, of Virginia, late a Chief Justice of the Nation, when it cracked without any apparent reason, while slowly tolling.

It once more left the city on January 23rd, 1885, for the New Orleans Exposition, and was returned to its place in the State House, on June 17th, 1885.

This miniature Bell will teach the young folks patriotism and economy, as it can be used for a Savings Bank for children, by breaking out the small piece of glass in the slot on the top of the Bell.

To OPEN.—Unscrew the base, place a plate thereon, reverse, slightly shake, remove and you will obtain a pretty jelly design fit for any table,

QUALITY—wholly pure, being made from grape juice, granulated sugar and choice wines.

In offering this beautiful design of a jelly glass and Savings Bank combined to the public, we feel justified in asking for your patronage.

Yours Very Respectfully,

ROBINSON & LOEBLE.

Patented May 15, 1951

Des. 163,307

UNITED STATES PATENT OFFICE

163,307

COIN BANK

Ralph Victor Moran, Bradford, Pa., assignor to
Vic Moran, Bradford, Pa., a partnership

Application November 18, 1947, Serial No. 142,602

Term of patent 14 years

(Cl. D34—11)

To all whom it may concern:

Be it known that I, Ralph Victor Moran, a citizen of the United States, residing at Bradford, in the county of McKean and Commonwealth of Pennsylvania, have invented a new, original, and ornamental Design for Coin Bank, of which the following is a specification, reference being had to the accompanying drawing, forming part thereof.

In the drawing:

Fig. 1 is a front elevational view of the coin bank, showing my new design;

Fig. 2 is a side elevational view thereof, partly in cross-section taken on the line 2—2 in Fig. 1; and

Fig. 3 is a top plan view thereof, partly in cross-section taken on the line 3—3 in Fig. 1.

The dominant features of my new design reside in the figure shown inside of the transparent globe.

I claim:

The ornamental design for a coin bank, as shown and described.

RALPH VICTOR MORAN.

REFERENCES CITED

The following references are of record in the file of this patent:

UNITED STATES PATENTS

Number	Name	Date
D. 124,655	Moran	Jan. 14, 1941
D. 147,899	Falk	Nov. 18, 1947
405,353	Hall	June 18, 1889
2,336,185	Moran	Dec. 7, 1943

May 15, 1951   R. V. MORAN   Des. 163,307

COIN BANK

Filed Nov. 18, 1947

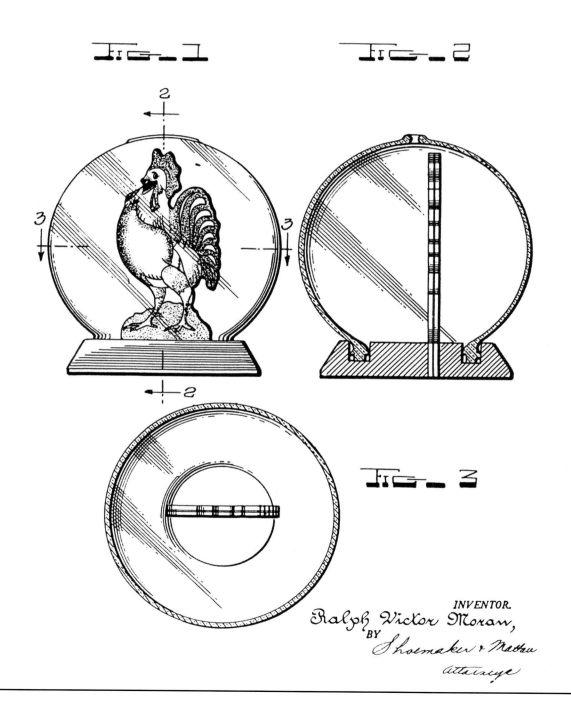

FIG_1   FIG_2

FIG_3

INVENTOR.

Ralph Victor Moran,

BY

Shoemaker & Mathew

attorneys

Patented May 15, 1951

Des. 163,309

UNITED STATES PATENT OFFICE

163,309

COIN BANK

Ralph Victor Moran, Bradford, Pa., assignor to
Vic Moran, Bradford, Pa., a partnership

Application November 18, 1947, Serial No. 142,605

Term of patent 14 years

(Cl. D34—11)

To all whom it may concern:

Be it known that I, Ralph Victor Moran, a citizen of the United States, residing at Bradford, in the county of McKean and Commonwealth of Pennsylvania, have invented a new, original, and ornamental Design for Coin Bank, of which the following is a specification, reference being had to the accompanying drawing, forming part thereof.

In the drawing:

Fig. 1 is a front elevational view of the coin bank, showing my new design;

Fig. 2 is a side elevational view thereof, partly in cross-section taken on the line 2—2 in Fig. 1; and

Fig. 3 is a top plan view thereof, partly in cross-section taken on the lines 3—3 in Fig. 1.

The dominant features of my new design reside in the figure shown inside of the transparent globe.

I claim:

The ornamental design for a coin bank, as shown and described.

RALPH VICTOR MORAN.

REFERENCES CITED

The following references are of record in the file of this patent:

UNITED STATES PATENTS

Number	Name	Date
2,336,185	Moran _____	Dec. 7, 1943

May 15, 1951   R. V. MORAN   Des. 163,309

COIN BANK

Filed Nov. 18, 1947

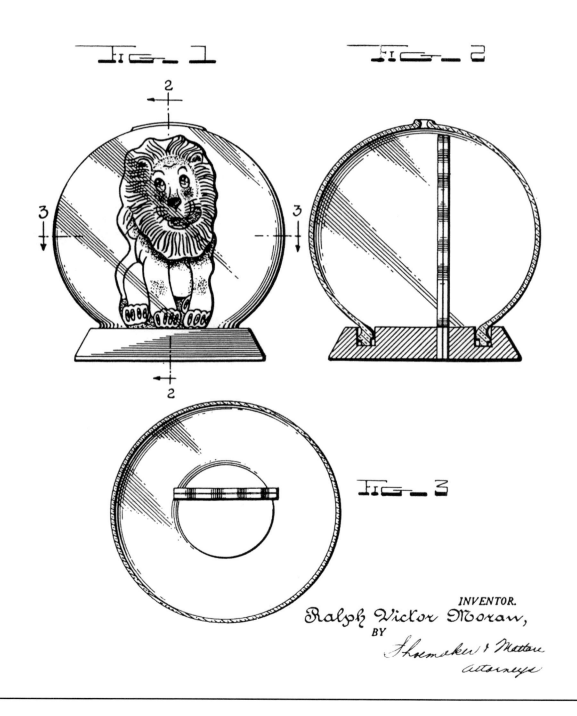

INVENTOR.

Ralph Victor Moran,

BY

Shoemaker & Mattare

attorneys

Patented May 15, 1951

Des. 163,310

UNITED STATES PATENT OFFICE

163,310

COIN BANK

Ralph Victor Moran, Bradford, Pa., assignor to
Vic Moran, Bradford, Pa., a partnership

Application November 18, 1947, Serial No. 142,606

Term of patent 14 years

(Cl. D34—11)

To all whom it may concern:

Be it known that I, Ralph Victor Moran, a citizen of the United States, residing at Bradford, in the county of McKean and Commonwealth of Pennsylvania, have invented a new, original, and ornamental Design for Coin Bank, of which the following is a specification, reference being had to the accompanying drawing, forming part thereof.

In the drawing:

Fig. 1 is a front elevational view of the coin bank, showing my new design;

Fig. 2 is a side elevational view thereof, partly in cross-section taken on the line 2—2 in Fig. 1; and

Fig. 3 is a top plan view thereof, partly in cross-section taken on the line 3—3 in Fig. 1.

The dominant features of my design reside in the figure shown inside of the transparent globe.

I claim:

The ornamental design for a coin bank, as shown and described.

RALPH VICTOR MORAN.

REFERENCES CITED

The following references are of record in the file of this patent:

UNITED STATES PATENTS

Number	Name	Date
D. 147,345	Moran	Aug. 19, 1947
2,336,185	Moran	Dec. 7, 1943

May 15, 1951   R. V. MORAN   Des. 163,310

COIN BANK

Filed Nov. 18, 1947

FIG_1

FIG_2

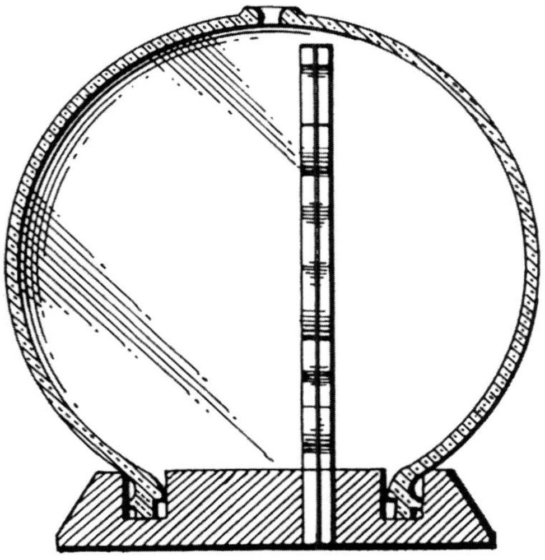

FIG_3

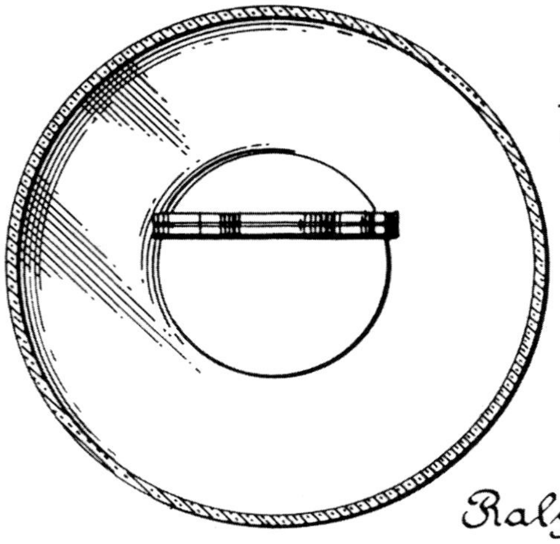

INVENTOR.

Ralph Victor Moran,

BY

Shoemaker & Mattare

Attorneys

UNITED STATES PATENT OFFICE.

WILLIAM M. KIRCHNER, OF PITTSBURG, PENNSYLVANIA.

IMPROVEMENT IN TOY MONEY-BANKS.

Specification forming part of Letters Patent No. **179,203**, dated June 27, 1876; application filed December 27, 1875.

To all whom it may concern:

Be it known that I, WILLIAM M. KIRCH-NER, of Pittsburg, county of Allegheny, State of Pennsylvania, have invented or discovered a new and useful Improvement in Manufacture of Glass Savings-Banks; and I do hereby declare the following to be a full, clear, concise, and exact description thereof, reference being had to the accompanying drawing, making a part of this specification, in which—like letters indicating like parts—

Figure 1 is a side elevation of my improvement in one of the many forms of its application. Fig. 2 is a transverse vertical section through *x x* of Fig. 1; and Fig. 3 is a longitudinal vertical section through *y y* of Fig. 2.

My improvement consists of a savings-bank, the ends, sides, and top of which are made in one piece of glass, and at one operation, with a suitable hole for making deposits. This glass part may be made of any desired form, but for the present purpose I have shown the bank made in imitation of Independence Hall. The sides A and ends A', as also the top, cover, or roof B, and the steeple B', (if such be made), are made of glass, by pressing or blowing the same in a suitable mold, all at one operation. By the use of a sliding bar or mandrel, which works through the mold cavity, a hole, *a*, is made for convenience in making deposits.

While the bottom D may be attached in various ways, I prefer that shown. A groove or recess, *s*, is made along the lower outer faces of the sides, and correspondingly-shaped tongues *s¹* on the side flanges *s²* of the bottom piece D enable the glass part A B to be slid into the bottom like a drawer. The bottom D is made of any suitable material, hard or seasoned wood answering the purpose. By trans-

verse keys *d d¹*, which engage a shoulder or rib, *d²*, on the ends A', and are seated in the bottom D, the body A B and bottom D are securely locked together. These transverse keys *d d¹*, sliding in end ways, are secured by screws, nails, or pins *c*, or in other suitable way.

For convenience in removing the deposits when desired, I make a recess, *n*, of suitable size in the lower edge of one end, so that it may be covered by the key *d* at that end, and also uncovered by sliding the key out. Hence the deposits can be removed without taking off the bottom.

I believe a savings-bank, having glass walls and cover made in one piece, with a hole therein for receiving deposits, to be an entirely new article, and, while not limiting myself to any particular or specific form, I believe the form shown to be one of those which will be most acceptable to the public.

I claim herein as my invention—

1. As a new article of manufacture, a toy money box or savings-bank, having glass walls and cover made in one piece, and with a hole therein for the reception of deposits, substantially as set forth.

2. In a toy money-box made of glass, as described, the recess *n*, for the removal of deposits, substantially as set forth.

3. The combination of glass body A B, bottom D, of wood or other material, with tongues and grooves, and transverse keys *d d¹*, substantially as set forth.

In testimony whereof I have hereunto set my hand.

WILLIAM M. KIRCHNER.

Witnesses:
JAMES M. CHRISTY,
GEO. H. CHRISTY.

INDEPENDENCE HALL

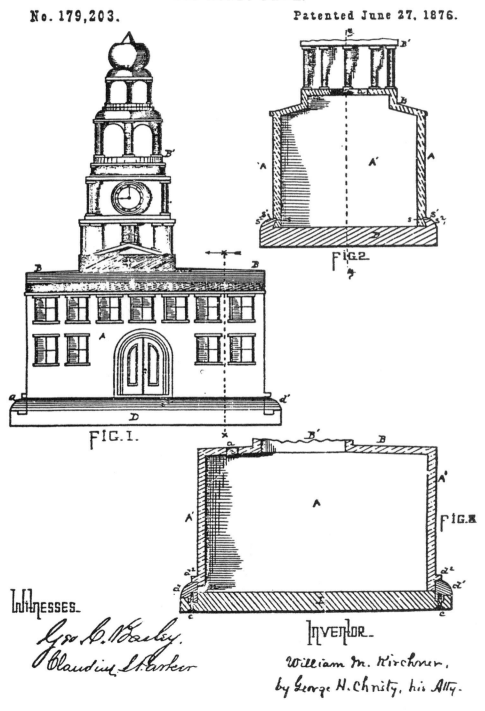

W. M. KIRCHNER.

TOY MONEY BANK.

No. 179,203.

Patented June 27, 1876.

FIG. I.

FIG. 2.

FIG. 3.

Witnesses

Geo. C. Bailey.

Claudius Parker

Inventor

William M. Kirchner.

by George H. Christy, his Atty.

# Bibliography

Books

Dezso, Douglas M., J. Leon and Rose D. Poirier. *Collector's Guide to Candy Containers, Identification and Values.* Paducah, Kentucky: Collector Books, 1998.

Duer, Don. *Penny Banks Around the World.* Atglen, Pennsylvania: Schiffer Publishing, Ltd., 1997.

Eikelberner, George, and Serge Agadjanian. *American Glass Candy Containers.* Privately published by Serge Agadjanian, Belle Mead, New Jersey, 1970 (out of print).

————. *More American Glass Candy Containers.* Privately published by Serge Agadjanian, Belle Mead, New Jersey, 1970 (out of print).

Long, Jeannie D. *An Album of Candy Containers.* Mokelumme Hill, California: Long's Americana, 1978.

————. *An Album of Candy Containers, Vol. II.* Kingsburg, California: Thomas O. Long and Jeannie D. Long, 1983.

Moore, Andy and Susan. *The Penny Bank Book.* Atglen, Pennsylvania: Schiffer, 1984.

Ostrander, Diane. *A Guide to American Nursing Bottles.* The American Collectors of Infant Feeders, Revised Edition, 1992.

Rogers, Carole. *Penny Banks, A History and a Handbook.* New York: E.P. Dutton, 1977 (out of print).

Periodicals

Camillo Jr., Carl. "Where Have all the Bubbles Gone?" history and information paper.

The Glass Bank Collectors Newsletter, Box 155, Poland, New York.

The Magazine of Old Glass, April, 1940, Vol. 4. . . No. 5, page 10.

Additional

Lids and closures for glass banks, Mike & Jo Baldwin, P.O. Box 2971, Anderson, Indiana 46018

About the Author

Charles V. Reynolds and his wife, Judy

Known to most as "Charlie," Charles V. Reynolds is a retired technology education teacher who has been in the toy business for over 30 years. Reynolds Toys, located in Falls Church, Virginia, is still a thriving family business, run by Charlie, his wife Judy, and their two sons, Jeff and Jason. The company produces new, original mechanical banks, still banks, and figural bottle openers in limited, numbered editions, as well as many other toys and novelties. Since 1964, Reynolds Toys has made 62 mechanical bank editions, 83 still bank editions, and 47 figural bottle opener editions.

Charlie Reynolds is the current president of the Mechanical Bank Collectors of America, and a member of the board of directors of the Still Bank Collectors Club. He is the advisor on country store items, figural bottle openers, and banks in *Schroeder's Antiques Price Guide*. Additionally, he is an active member of the Train Collectors Association, Mid-Atlantic Penny Bank Club, Figural Bottle Opener Club, Kollectors of Old Kitchen Stuff, Candy Container Collectors of America, and Antique Toy Collectors of America.

Charlie and his wife, Judy, claim to be crazy collectors, and who could argue? Besides their adoration of bank collecting, they love to accumulate country store items such as string holders, tobacco plug cutters, advertising trade cards, laundry irons, figural nutcrackers, pencil sharpeners, soda fountain items, antique toy trains and other railroad items, miniature figural skillets, teddy bears, Beatrix Potter figures, Santa Claus figures, and Dickens Village pieces. They keep themselves very busy with hobbies.

COLLECTOR BOOKS

Informing Today's Collector

For over two decades we have been keeping collectors informed on trends and values in all fields of antiques and collectibles.

DOLLS, FIGURES & TEDDY BEARS

4707	A Decade of **Barbie Dolls** & Collectibles, 1981–1991, Summers	$19.95
4631	**Barbie Doll** Boom, 1986–1995, Augustyniak	$18.95
2079	**Barbie Doll** Fashion, Volume I, Eames	$24.95
4846	**Barbie Doll** Fashion, Volume II, Eames	$24.95
3957	**Barbie** Exclusives, Rana	$18.95
4632	**Barbie** Exclusives, Book II, Rana	$18.95
4557	**Barbie,** The First 30 Years, Deutsch	$24.95
5672	The **Barbie Doll** Years, 4th Ed., Olds	$19.95
3810	**Chatty Cathy** Dolls, Lewis	$15.95
5352	Collector's Ency. of **Barbie** Doll Exclusives & More, 2nd Ed.,Augustyniak	$24.95
2211	Collector's Encyclopedia of **Madame Alexander** Dolls, Smith	$24.95
4863	Collector's Encyclopedia of **Vogue Dolls**, Izen/Stover	$29.95
5598	**Doll Values**, Antique to Modern, 4th Ed., Moyer	$12.95
56101	**Madame Alexander** Collector's Dolls Price Guide #25, Crowsey	$9.95
5612	**Modern Collectible Dolls**, Volume IV, Moyer	$24.95
5365	**Peanuts Collectibles**, Podley/Bang	$24.95
5253	Story of **Barbie**, 2nd Ed., Westenhouser	$24.95
5277	**Talking Toys** of the 20th Century, Lewis	$15.95
1513	**Teddy Bears & Steiff** Animals, Mandel	$9.95
1817	**Teddy Bears & Steiff** Animals, 2nd Series, Mandel	$19.95
2084	**Teddy Bears, Annalee's & Steiff** Animals, 3rd Series, Mandel	$19.95
5371	**Teddy Bear** Treasury, Yenke	$19.95
1808	Wonder of **Barbie**, Manos	$9.95
1430	World of **Barbie** Dolls, Manos	$9.95
4880	World of **Raggedy Ann** Collectibles, Avery	$24.95

TOYS, MARBLES & CHRISTMAS COLLECTIBLES

2333	Antique & Collectible **Marbles**, 3rd Ed., Grist	$9.95
5353	**Breyer Animal** Collector's Guide, 2nd Ed., Browell	$19.95
4976	**Christmas Ornaments**, Lights & Decorations, Johnson	$24.95
4737	**Christmas Ornaments**, Lights & Decorations, Vol. II, Johnson	$24.95
4739	**Christmas Ornaments**, Lights & Decorations, Vol. III, Johnson	$24.95
4649	Classic Plastic **Model Kits**, Polizzi	$24.95
4559	Collectible **Action Figures**, 2nd Ed., Manos	$17.95
3874	Collectible **Coca-Cola Toy Trucks**, deCourtivron	$24.95
2338	Collector's Encyclopedia of **Disneyana**, Longest, Stern	$24.95
4958	Collector's Guide to **Battery Toys**, Hultzman	$19.95
5038	Collector's Guide to **Diecast Toys** & Scale Models, 2nd Ed., Johnson	$19.95
4651	Collector's Guide to **Tinker Toys**, Strange	$18.95
4566	Collector's Guide to **Tootsietoys**, 2nd Ed., Richter	$19.95
5169	Collector's Guide to **TV Toys** & Memorabilia, 2nd Ed., Davis/Morgan	$24.95
5360	**Fisher-Price Toys**, Cassity	$19.95
4720	The Golden Age of **Automotive Toys**, 1925–1941, Hutchison/Johnson	$24.95
5593	**Grist's** Big Book of **Marbles**, 2nd Ed.	$24.95
3970	**Grist's** Machine-Made & Contemporary **Marbles**, 2nd Ed.	$9.95
5267	**Matchbox Toys**, 1947 to 1998, 3rd Ed., Johnson	$19.95
4871	**McDonald's** Collectibles, Henriques/DuVall	$19.95
1540	**Modern Toys** 1930–1980, Baker	$19.95
3888	**Motorcycle Toys**, Antique & Contemporary, Gentry/Downs	$18.95
5368	**Schroeder's Collectible Toys**, Antique to Modern Price Guide, 6th Ed.	$17.95
2028	**Toys**, Antique & Collectible, Longest	$14.95

FURNITURE

1457	American **Oak** Furniture, McNerney	$9.95
3716	American **Oak** Furniture, Book II, McNerney	$12.95
1118	Antique **Oak** Furniture, Hill	$7.95
2271	Collector's Encyclopedia of **American** Furniture, Vol. II, Swedberg	$24.95
3720	Collector's Encyclopedia of **American** Furniture, Vol. III, Swedberg	$24.95
5359	Early **American** Furniture, Obbard	$12.95
1755	Furniture of the **Depression Era**, Swedberg	$19.95
3906	**Heywood-Wakefield** Modern Furniture, Rouland	$18.95
1885	**Victorian** Furniture, Our American Heritage, McNerney	$9.95

3829	**Victorian** Furniture, Our American Heritage, Book II, McNerney	$9.95

JEWELRY, HATPINS, WATCHES & PURSES

1712	Antique & Collectible **Thimbles** & Accessories, Mathis	$19.95
1748	Antique **Purses**, Revised Second Ed., Holiner	$19.95
1278	Art Nouveau & Art Deco **Jewelry**, Baker	$9.95
4850	Collectible **Costume Jewelry**, Simonds	$24.95
3722	Collector's Ency. of **Compacts**, Carryalls & Face Powder Boxes, Mueller	$24.95
4940	**Costume Jewelry**, A Practical Handbook & Value Guide, Rezazadeh	$24.95
1716	Fifty Years of Collectible **Fashion Jewelry**, 1925–1975, Baker	$19.95
1424	**Hatpins** & Hatpin Holders, Baker	$9.95
1181	100 Years of Collectible **Jewelry**, 1850–1950, Baker	$9.95
4729	**Sewing Tools** & Trinkets, Thompson	$24.95
5620	Unsigned Beauties of **Costume Jewelry**, Brown	$24.95
4878	Vintage & Contemporary **Purse Accessories**, Gerson	$24.95
3830	Vintage **Vanity Bags** & Purses, Gerson	$24.95

INDIANS, GUNS, KNIVES, TOOLS, PRIMITIVES

1868	Antique **Tools**, Our American Heritage, McNerney	$9.95
5616	Big Book of **Pocket Knives**, Stewart	$19.95
4943	Field Guide to Flint **Arrowheads** & **Knives** of the North American Indian	$9.95
3885	**Indian Artifacts** of the Midwest, Book II, Hothem	$16.95
4870	**Indian Artifacts** of the Midwest, Book III, Hothem	$18.95
5685	**Indian Artifacts** of the Midwest, Book IV, Hothem	$19.95
5687	**Modern Guns**, Identification & Values, 13th Ed., Quertermous	$14.95
2164	**Primitives**, Our American Heritage, McNerney	$9.95
1759	**Primitives**, Our American Heritage, 2nd Series, McNerney	$14.95
4730	Standard **Knife** Collector's Guide, 3rd Ed., Ritchie & Stewart	$12.95

PAPER COLLECTIBLES & BOOKS

4633	**Big Little Books**, Jacobs	$18.95
4710	Collector's Guide to **Children's Books**, 1850 to 1950, Jones	$18.95
5596	Collector's Guide to **Children's Books**, 1950 to 1975, Jones	$19.95
1441	Collector's Guide to **Post Cards**, Wood	$9.95
2081	Guide to Collecting **Cookbooks**, Allen	$14.95
5613	Huxford's **Old Book** Value Guide, 12th Ed.	$19.95
2080	Price Guide to **Cookbooks** & Recipe Leaflets, Dickinson	$9.95
3973	**Sheet Music** Reference & Price Guide, 2nd Ed., Pafik & Guiheen	$19.95
4654	**Victorian Trade Cards**, Historical Reference & Value Guide, Cheadle	$19.95
4733	**Whitman Juvenile Books**, Brown	$17.95

GLASSWARE

5602	Anchor Hocking's **Fire-King** & More, 2nd Ed.	$24.95
4561	Collectible **Drinking Glasses**, Chase & Kelly	$17.95
4642	Collectible **Glass Shoes**, Wheatley	$19.95
5357	Coll. **Glassware** from the 40s, 50s & 60s, 5th Ed., Florence	$19.95
1810	Collector's Encyclopedia of **American Art Glass**, Shuman	$29.95
5358	Collector's Encyclopedia of **Depression Glass**, 14th Ed., Florence	$19.95
1961	Collector's Encyclopedia of **Fry Glassware**, Fry Glass Society	$24.95
1664	Collector's Encyclopedia of **Heisey Glass**, 1925–1938, Bredehoft	$24.95
3905	Collector's Encyclopedia of **Milk Glass**, Newbound	$24.95
4936	Collector's Guide to **Candy Containers**, Dezso/Poirier	$19.95
4564	**Crackle Glass**, Weitman	$19.95
4941	**Crackle Glass**, Book II, Weitman	$19.95
4714	**Czechoslovakian Glass** and Collectibles, Book II, Barta/Rose	$16.95
5528	Early American **Pattern Glass**, Metz	$17.95
5682	**Elegant Glassware** of the Depression Era, 9th Ed., Florence	$19.95
5614	Field Guide to **Pattern Glass**, McCain	$17.95
3981	Evers' Standard **Cut Glass** Value Guide	$12.95
4659	**Fenton** Art Glass, 1907–1939, Whitmyer	$24.95
5615	Florence's **Glassware Pattern Identification** Guide, Vol. II	$19.95
3725	**Fostoria**, Pressed, Blown & Hand Molded Shapes, Kerr	$24.95
4719	**Fostoria**, Etched, Carved & Cut Designs, Vol. II, Kerr	$24.95

COLLECTOR BOOKS
Informing Today's Collector

3883	**Fostoria Stemware**, The Crystal for America, Long/Seate	$24.95
5261	**Fostoria Tableware**, 1924 – 1943, Long/Seate	$24.95
5361	**Fostoria Tableware**, 1944 – 1986, Long/Seate	$24.95
5604	**Fostoria**, Useful & Ornamental, Long/Seate	$29.95
4644	**Imperial Carnival Glass**, Burns	$18.95
3886	**Kitchen Glassware** of the Depression Years, 5th Ed., Florence	$19.95
5600	Much More Early American **Pattern Glass**, Metz	$17.95
5690	Pocket Guide to **Depression Glass**, 12th Ed., Florence	$9.95
5594	Standard Encyclopedia of **Carnival Glass**, 7th Ed., Edwards/Carwile	$29.95
5595	Standard **Carnival Glass** Price Guide, 12th Ed., Edwards/Carwile	$9.95
5272	Standard Encyclopedia of **Opalescent Glass**, 3rd Ed., Edwards/Carwile	$24.95
5617	Standard Encyclopedia of **Pressed Glass**, 2nd Ed., Edwards/Carwile	$29.95
4731	**Stemware Identification**, Featuring Cordials with Values, Florence	$24.95
4732	**Very Rare Glassware** of the Depression Years, 5th Series, Florence	$24.95
4656	**Westmoreland Glass**, Wilson	$24.95

POTTERY

4927	**ABC Plates & Mugs**, Lindsay	$24.95
4929	**American Art Pottery**, Sigafoose	$24.95
4630	**American Limoges**, Limoges	$24.95
1312	**Blue & White Stoneware**, McNerney	$9.95
1958	So. Potteries **Blue Ridge Dinnerware**, 3rd Ed., Newbound	$14.95
1959	**Blue Willow**, 2nd Ed., Gaston	$14.95
4851	Collectible **Cups & Saucers**, Harran	$18.95
1373	Collector's Encyclopedia of **American Dinnerware**, Cunningham	$24.95
4931	Collector's Encyclopedia of **Bauer Pottery**, Chipman	$24.95
4932	Collector's Encyclopedia of **Blue Ridge Dinnerware**, Vol. II, Newbound	$24.95
4658	Collector's Encyclopedia of **Brush-McCoy Pottery**, Huxford	$24.95
5034	Collector's Encyclopedia of **California Pottery**, 2nd Ed., Chipman	$24.95
2133	Collector's Encyclopedia of **Cookie Jars**, Roerig	$24.95
3723	Collector's Encyclopedia of **Cookie Jars**, Book II, Roerig	$24.95
4939	Collector's Encyclopedia of **Cookie Jars**, Book III, Roerig	$24.95
5040	Collector's Encyclopedia of **Fiesta**, 8th Ed., Huxford	$19.95
4718	Collector's Encyclopedia of **Figural Planters & Vases**, Newbound	$19.95
3961	Collector's Encyclopedia of **Early Noritake**, Alden	$24.95
1439	Collector's Encyclopedia of **Flow Blue China**, Gaston	$19.95
3812	Collector's Encyclopedia of **Flow Blue China**, 2nd Ed., Gaston	$24.95
3431	Collector's Encyclopedia of **Homer Laughlin China**, Jasper	$24.95
1276	Collector's Encyclopedia of **Hull Pottery**, Roberts	$19.95
3962	Collector's Encyclopedia of **Lefton China**, DeLozier	$19.95
4855	Collector's Encyclopedia of **Lefton China**, Book II, DeLozier	$19.95
5609	Collector's Encyclopedia of **Limoges Porcelain**, 3rd Ed., Gaston	$24.95
2334	Collector's Encyclopedia of **Majolica Pottery**, Katz-Marks	$19.95
1358	Collector's Encyclopedia of **McCoy Pottery**, Huxford	$19.95
3837	Collector's Encyclopedia of **Nippon Porcelain**, Van Patten	$24.95
2089	Collector's Ency. of **Nippon Porcelain**, 2nd Series, Van Patten	$24.95
1665	Collector's Ency. of **Nippon Porcelain**, 3rd Series, Van Patten	$24.95
4712	Collector's Ency. of **Nippon Porcelain**, 4th Series, Van Patten	$24.95
1447	Collector's Encyclopedia of **Noritake**, Van Patten	$19.95
1037	Collector's Encyclopedia of **Occupied Japan**, 1st Series, Florence	$14.95
1038	Collector's Encyclopedia of **Occupied Japan**, 2nd Series, Florence	$14.95
2335	Collector's Encyclopedia of **Occupied Japan**, 5th Series, Florence	$14.95
4951	Collector's Encyclopedia of **Old Ivory China**, Hillman	$24.95
5564	Collector's Encyclopedia of **Pickard China**, Reed	$29.95
3877	Collector's Encyclopedia of **R.S. Prussia**, 4th Series, Gaston	$24.95
5618	Collector's Encyclopedia of **Rosemeade Pottery**, Dommel	$24.95
1034	Collector's Encyclopedia of **Roseville Pottery**, Huxford	$19.95
1035	Collector's Encyclopedia of **Roseville Pottery**, 2nd Ed., Huxford	$19.95
4856	Collector's Encyclopedia of **Russel Wright**, 2nd Ed., Kerr	$24.95
4713	Collector's Encyclopedia of **Salt Glaze Stoneware**, Taylor/Lowrance	$24.95
3314	Collector's Encyclopedia of **Van Briggle Art Pottery**, Sasicki	$24.95
4563	Collector's Encyclopedia of **Wall Pockets**, Newbound	$19.95
2111	Collector's Encyclopedia of **Weller Pottery**, Huxford	$29.95
3876	Collector's Guide to **Lu-Ray Pastels**, Meehan	$18.95
3814	Collector's Guide to **Made in Japan Ceramics**, White	$18.95

4646	Collector's Guide to **Made in Japan Ceramics**, Book II, White	$18.95
2339	Collector's Guide to **Shawnee Pottery**, Vanderbilt	$19.95
1425	**Cookie Jars**, Westfall	$9.95
3440	**Cookie Jars**, Book II, Westfall	$19.95
4924	Figural & Novelty **Salt & Pepper Shakers**, 2nd Series, Davern	$24.95
2379	Lehner's Ency. of **U.S. Marks** on Pottery, Porcelain & China	$24.95
4722	**McCoy Pottery**, Collector's Reference & Value Guide, Hanson/Nissen	$19.95
1670	**Red Wing Collectibles**, DePasquale	$9.95
1440	**Red Wing Stoneware**, DePasquale	$9.95
1632	**Salt & Pepper Shakers**, Guarnaccia	$9.95
5091	**Salt & Pepper Shakers** II, Guarnaccia	$18.95
2220	**Salt & Pepper Shakers** III, Guarnaccia	$14.95
3443	**Salt & Pepper Shakers** IV, Guarnaccia	$18.95
3738	**Shawnee Pottery**, Mangus	$24.95
4629	Turn of the Century **American Dinnerware**, 1880s–1920s, Jasper	$24.95
3327	**Watt Pottery** – Identification & Value Guide, Morris	$19.95

OTHER COLLECTIBLES

4704	Antique & Collectible **Buttons**, Wisniewski	$19.95
2269	Antique **Brass & Copper** Collectibles, Gaston	$16.95
1880	Antique **Iron**, McNerney	$9.95
3872	Antique **Tins**, Dodge	$24.95
4845	Antique **Typewriters & Office Collectibles**, Rehr	$19.95
5607	Antiquing and Collecting on the **Internet**, Parry	$12.95
1128	**Bottle** Pricing Guide, 3rd Ed., Cleveland	$7.95
4636	**Celluloid** Collectibles, Dunn	$14.95
3718	Collectible **Aluminum**, Grist	$16.95
4560	Collectible **Cats**, An Identification & Value Guide, Book II, Fyke	$19.95
4852	Collectible **Compact Disc** Price Guide 2, Cooper	$17.95
5666	Collector's Encyclopedia of **Granite Ware**, Book 2, Greguire	$29.95
4705	Collector's Guide to **Antique Radios**, 4th Ed., Bunis	$18.95
5608	Collector's Gde. to Buying, Selling, & Trading on the **Internet**, 2nd Ed., Hix	$12.95
3880	Collector's Guide to **Cigarette Lighters**, Flanagan	$17.95
4637	Collector's Guide to **Cigarette Lighters**, Book II, Flanagan	$17.95
4942	Collector's Guide to **Don Winton Designs**, Ellis	$19.95
3966	Collector's Guide to **Inkwells**, Identification & Values, Badders	$18.95
4947	Collector's Guide to **Inkwells**, Book II, Badders	$19.95
5621	Collector's Guide to **Online Auctions**, Hix	$12.95
4862	Collector's Guide to **Toasters** & Accessories, Greguire	$19.95
4652	Collector's Guide to **Transistor Radios**, 2nd Ed., Bunis	$16.95
4864	Collector's Guide to **Wallace Nutting Pictures**, Ivankovich	$18.95
1629	**Doorstops**, Identification & Values, Bertoia	$9.95
4717	Figural **Nodders**, Includes Bobbin' Heads and Swayers, Irtz	$19.95
5683	**Fishing Lure** Collectibles, 2nd Ed., Murphy/Edmisten	$29.95
5259	**Flea Market Trader**, 12th Ed., Huxford	$9.95
4945	**G-Men and FBI Toys** and Collectibles, Whitworth	$18.95
5605	**Garage Sale & Flea Market Annual**, 8th Ed.	$19.95
3819	**General Store** Collectibles, Wilson	$24.95
5159	Huxford's Collectible **Advertising**, 4th Ed.	$24.95
2216	**Kitchen Antiques**, 1790–1940, McNerney	$14.95
4950	The **Lone Ranger**, Collector's Reference & Value Guide, Felbinger	$18.95
2026	**Railroad** Collectibles, 4th Ed., Baker	$14.95
5619	**Roy Rogers and Dale Evans** Toys & Memorabilia, Coyle	$24.95
5367	**Schroeder's Antiques Price Guide**, 18th Ed., Huxford	$12.95
5007	**Silverplated Flatware**, Revised 4th Edition, Hagan	$18.95
1922	Standard **Old Bottle** Price Guide, Sellari	$14.95
5694	**Summers' Guide to Coca-Cola**, 3rd Ed.	$24.95
5356	**Summers' Pocket Guide to Coca-Cola**, 2nd Ed.	$9.95
3892	**Toy & Miniature Sewing Machines**, Thomas	$18.95
4876	**Toy & Miniature Sewing Machines**, Book II, Thomas	$24.95
5144	Value Guide to **Advertising Memorabilia**, 2nd Ed., Summers	$19.95
3977	Value Guide to **Gas Station Memorabilia**, Summers & Priddy	$24.95
4877	Vintage **Bar Ware**, Visakay	$24.95
4935	The W.F. Cody **Buffalo Bill** Collector's Guide with Values	$24.95
5281	**Wanted to Buy**, 7th Edition	$9.95

Schroeder's
ANTIQUES
Price Guide

. . . is the #1 bestselling antiques & collectibles value guide on the market today, and here's why . . .

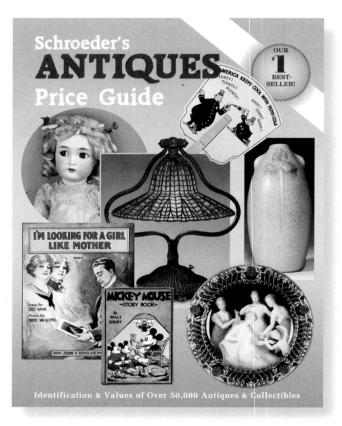

Identification & Values of Over 50,000 Antiques & Collectibles

8½ x 11, 608 Pages, $14.95

• *More than 450 advisors, well-known dealers, and top-notch collectors work together with our editors to bring you accurate information regarding pricing and identification.*

• *More than 45,000 items in almost 550 categories are listed along with hundreds of sharp original photos that illustrate not only the rare and unusual, but the common, popular collectibles as well.*

• *Each large close-up shot shows important details clearly. Every subject is represented with histories and background information, a feature not found in any of our competitors' publications.*

• *Our editors keep abreast of newly developing trends, often adding several new categories a year as the need arises.*

If it merits the interest of today's collector, you'll find it in *Schroeder's*. And you can feel confident that the information we publish is up to date and accurate. Our advisors thoroughly check each category to spot inconsistencies, listings that may not be entirely reflective of market dealings, and lines too vague to be of merit. Only the best of the lot remains for publication.

Collector Books
P.O. Box 3009
Paducah, KY 42002-3009
1-800-626-5420
www.collectorbooks.com

COLLECTOR BOOKS
A Division of Schroeder Publishing Co., Inc.